P9-DNR-124

SEW IT,
STUFF IT

SEW IT, STUFF IT

Cut, stitch, and sew 25 adorable soft toys

Rob Merrett

CICO BOOKS

LONDON NEW YORK

DEDICATION
This book is dedicated to Luisa Pardo de Benito and Philip Baker-Davey. And in memory of the deep love and precious times we once shared. Remembering you both is easy. I do it every day.

Published in 2010 by CICO Books
An imprint of Ryland Peters & Small Ltd
20–21 Jockey's Fields, London WC1R 4BW
519 Broadway, 5th Floor, New York NY 10012

www.cicobooks.com

10 9 8 7 6 5 4 3 2 1

Text copyright © Rob Merrett 2010
Design, illustration, and photography
copyright © CICO Books 2010

The author's moral rights have been asserted.
All rights reserved. No part of this publication
may be reproduced, stored in a retrieval
system, or transmitted in any form or by any
means, electronic, mechanical, photocopying,
or otherwise, without the prior permission of
the publisher.

A CIP catalog record for this book is
available from the Library of Congress
and the British Library.

ISBN: 978 1 907030 60 4

Printed in China

Editor: **Sarah Hoggett**
Design: **Elizabeth Healey**
Illustration: **Kate Simunek**
Photography: **Emma Mitchell**
Art direction and styling: **Luis Peral**

Contents

Introduction

Today, alongside more traditional soft toys for young children, there are a multitude of new and exciting playthings from around the world, readily available to buy in "a store near you!" They are full of originality and are no doubt destined to become a special friend to a little girl or boy. However, they are often one of many, churned out in their hundreds, thousands, tens of thousands even. So maybe they're not that special after all?

To me, the important difference between the toys made for sale on the high street and the ones featured in this book is that the latter will be made with love, and probably made with a very special little person in mind. A toy fashioned by your own hands possesses so much more character. A handmade gift has and always will be appreciated so much more, because making a gift for a baby, small child or anyone, for that matter, is a true expression of love.

This book is also about encouraging the reader to learn skills once traditionally taught at home—sewing, stitching, and embroidering. It's about expressing your individuality: no two toys will ever be alike and you can personalize them still further by embroidering a monogram or adding your own decorative appliqués to appeal to a child's imagination. It's about re-using and re-cycling, and I encourage you to embellish your toys with vintage fabric scraps from clothing cast-offs and to make dolls' dresses from old, worn tablecloths and napkins; even a remnant with a simple row of embroidered stitches adds charm to a stuffed toy. For older children, decorate the toys with broken jewelry, odd buttons, and objects found in flea markets, thrift stores, and garage sales.

In this book you will find plenty of affordable ideas and inspiration for enchanting gifts and keepsakes that I hope will become tomorrow's childhood treasures. There are cute creatures ranging from simple

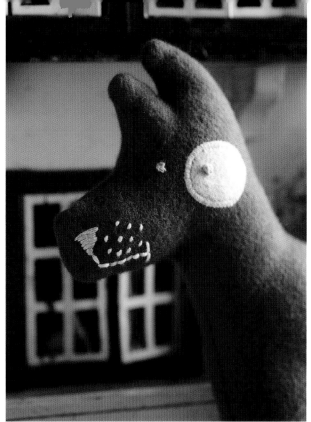
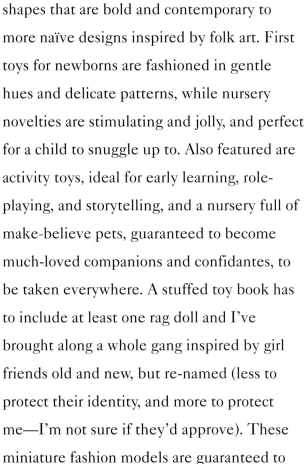

shapes that are bold and contemporary to more naïve designs inspired by folk art. First toys for newborns are fashioned in gentle hues and delicate patterns, while nursery novelties are stimulating and jolly, and perfect for a child to snuggle up to. Also featured are activity toys, ideal for early learning, role-playing, and storytelling, and a nursery full of make-believe pets, guaranteed to become much-loved companions and confidantes, to be taken everywhere. A stuffed toy book has to include at least one rag doll and I've brought along a whole gang inspired by girl friends old and new, but re-named (less to protect their identity, and more to protect me—I'm not sure if they'd approve). These miniature fashion models are guaranteed to

appeal to both the young and the young-at-heart. My mum, now an octogenarian but just as petite and feminine as she was in the 1940s when she was a mere slip of a thing, still cannot resist giving my sister's long-abandoned dolls elaborate pin curls, "Victory rolls," and munitions factory-style hairdos—so all the girls in the group have fine heads of "hair" to play with and re-style.

I have spent many happy hours making this eclectic bunch, inventing their personalities, and planning their adventures. Sewn into the very fabric are my childhood memories, present thoughts, and future hopes. I hope you, too, will embark on an equally pleasurable and satisfying journey as you take up your needle and thread. Happy sewing!

1. Baby's first soft toy

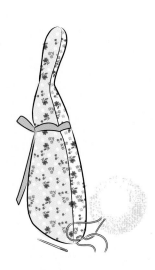

DAISY THE DINOSAUR

This prehistoric animal has captured the imagination of little boys and girls alike and no collection of children's toys, games, or books is worth its salt without one —so, say hello to Daisy. I'll admit she's not very scary—but she is cool! With her flower-power eyes and a pretty daisy chain resting on her rump, she's the ultimate '60s flower child.

YOU WILL NEED

- Pattern A1 from the pull-out sheet
- 13½ x 36 in. (34 x 90 cm) spotted fabric for body
- 2 in. (5 cm) jumbo rickrack for tongue
- 12 in. (30 cm) white floral trim
- Felt scraps for eyes and nostrils
- Hollow fiber filling

Other stuff

- Sewing machine
- Needle and matching sewing threads
- Glue gun or fabric glue
- Hole punch

- Take ⅜-in. (1-cm) seam allowances throughout unless otherwise stated.

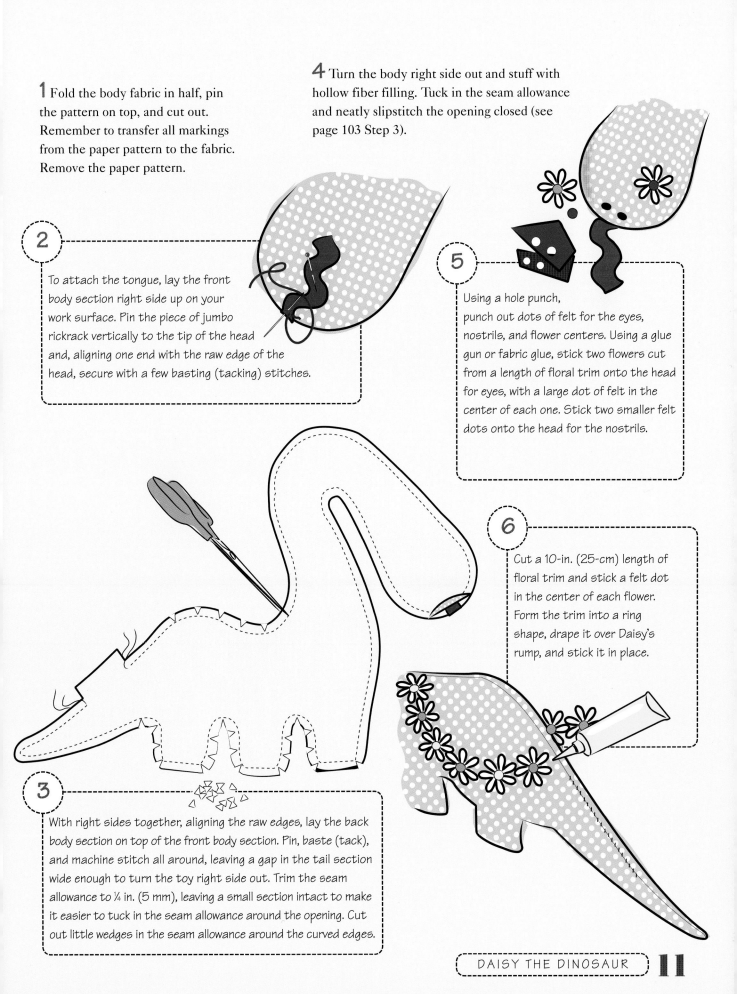

1 Fold the body fabric in half, pin the pattern on top, and cut out. Remember to transfer all markings from the paper pattern to the fabric. Remove the paper pattern.

4 Turn the body right side out and stuff with hollow fiber filling. Tuck in the seam allowance and neatly slipstitch the opening closed (see page 103 Step 3).

2 To attach the tongue, lay the front body section right side up on your work surface. Pin the piece of jumbo rickrack vertically to the tip of the head and, aligning one end with the raw edge of the head, secure with a few basting (tacking) stitches.

5 Using a hole punch, punch out dots of felt for the eyes, nostrils, and flower centers. Using a glue gun or fabric glue, stick two flowers cut from a length of floral trim onto the head for eyes, with a large dot of felt in the center of each one. Stick two smaller felt dots onto the head for the nostrils.

6 Cut a 10-in. (25-cm) length of floral trim and stick a felt dot in the center of each flower. Form the trim into a ring shape, drape it over Daisy's rump, and stick it in place.

3 With right sides together, aligning the raw edges, lay the back body section on top of the front body section. Pin, baste (tack), and machine stitch all around, leaving a gap in the tail section wide enough to turn the toy right side out. Trim the seam allowance to ¼ in. (5 mm), leaving a small section intact to make it easier to tuck in the seam allowance around the opening. Cut out little wedges in the seam allowance around the curved edges.

MATRYOSHKA BUNNIES

An elegant quartet of perfectly poised rabbits, made in decreasing sizes to gently watch over your little one asleep in the nursery. This simple design allows the dainty fabrics to shine through. Sporting tinkling bells and jaunty satin ribbons around their necks, this sophisticated set makes an enchanting gift for an Easter baby and is destined to become a cherished family heirloom.

YOU WILL NEED

- Pattern B1 from the pull-out sheet
  Note: The pattern on the pull-out sheet is for the smallest rabbit. To complete the quartet, simply enlarge it by 125, 145, and 170 percent in turn.
- 20 in. (50 cm) floral print fabric, 44 in. (112 cm) wide, for four rabbit fronts
- 20 in. (50 cm) contrast floral print fabric, 44 in. (112 cm) wide, for four rabbit backs
- Two 2-oz (50-g) balls pure wool light worsted (double knitting) yarn, for four pompoms

- Four 40-in. (100-cm) lengths of satin ribbon, ½ in. (10 mm) wide, for neck bows
- Four round silver bells
- Brown stranded embroidery floss (cotton)
- Scraps of brown felt for eyes
- Hollow fiber filling

Other stuff
- Sewing machine
- Needle and matching sewing threads

- Take ⅜-in. (1-cm) seam allowances throughout unless otherwise stated.

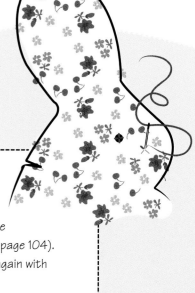

1 Place the two floral fabrics right sides together. Pin the pattern to the fabric and cut out. Lightly transfer the face markings onto the right side of the front body piece and make a snip in the seam allowance to show where the neck ribbon is to be attached. Remove the paper pattern.

2 Cut out the eyes from scraps of brown felt and stitch them in place with a star stitch (see page 104). Embroider the mouth, again with a single star stitch.

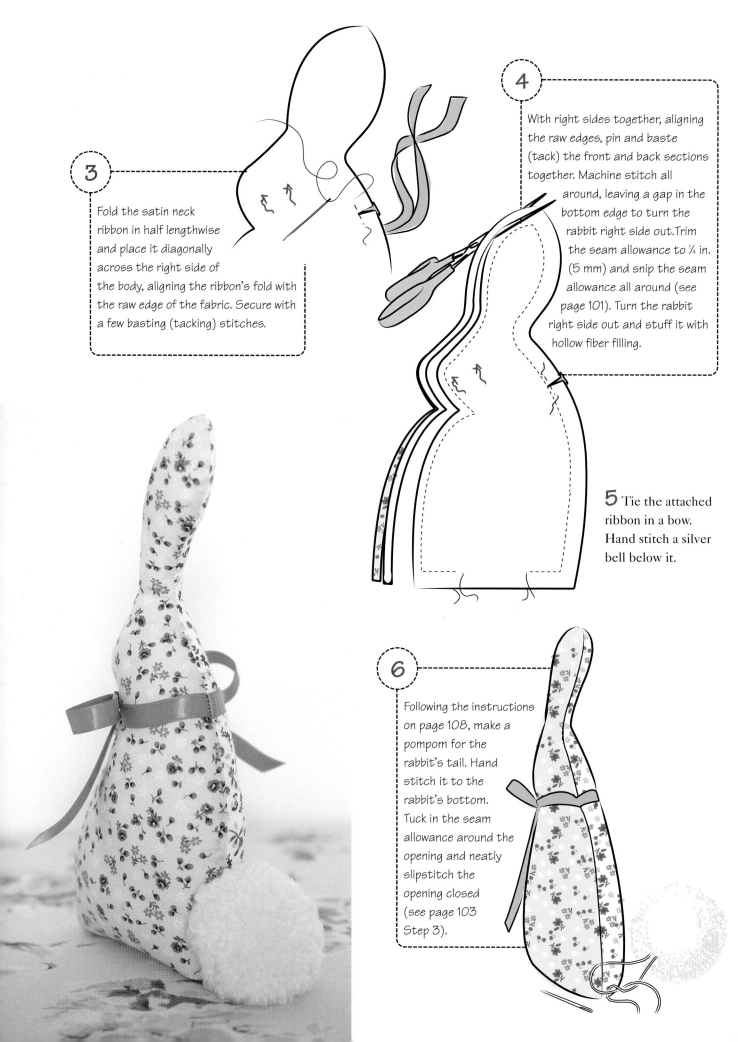

3 Fold the satin neck ribbon in half lengthwise and place it diagonally across the right side of the body, aligning the ribbon's fold with the raw edge of the fabric. Secure with a few basting (tacking) stitches.

4 With right sides together, aligning the raw edges, pin and baste (tack) the front and back sections together. Machine stitch all around, leaving a gap in the bottom edge to turn the rabbit right side out. Trim the seam allowance to ¼ in. (5 mm) and snip the seam allowance all around (see page 101). Turn the rabbit right side out and stuff it with hollow fiber filling.

5 Tie the attached ribbon in a bow. Hand stitch a silver bell below it.

6 Following the instructions on page 108, make a pompom for the rabbit's tail. Hand stitch it to the rabbit's bottom. Tuck in the seam allowance around the opening and neatly slipstitch the opening closed (see page 103 Step 3).

MARVIN THE MOUSE

Marvin reminds me of the sugar mouse I always used to find at the bottom of my Christmas stocking—and he's just as sweet. He's a stocky little critter and ever so cuddly in soft white cotton gabardine and fondant pink felt. Why not make three of him? Replace the beady black eyes with simple cross stitches and you have the characters from the famous English rhyme, "Three Blind Mice."

YOU WILL NEED

- Pattern pieces C1–C4 and templates C1–C3 from the pull-out sheet
- 12 x 21½ in. (30 x 54 cm) white cotton gabardine for body, base, and ears
- 4 x 12 in. (10 x 30 cm) pink felt for belly, inner ears, feet, and tail
- Pink and black stranded embroidery floss (cotton) for mouth and whiskers
- Black felt scraps for eyes
- Fusible bonding web
- Hollow fiber filling

Other stuff

- Sewing machine
- Needle and matching sewing threads
- Hole punch
- Glue

- Take ⅜-in. (1-cm) seam allowances throughout unless otherwise stated.

1 Pin the paper pattern pieces to the fabric and cut out two front and two back bodies, four ears, and one base. Remove the paper patterns.

2 Run a short row of machine stitches ⅜ in. (1 cm) in from what will be the center back seam of both back body pieces as a guide for when finishing the toy after stuffing (see page 103).

4 Draw around the inner ear template twice on the pink felt, and cut out. Aligning the straight edges, lay one inner ear on one cotton ear and appliqué it in place (see page 105). With right sides together, lay a second cotton ear on the appliquéd ear. Pin, baste (tack), and machine stitch all the way around, leaving the straight edge open. Trim the seam allowance to ¼ in. (5 mm), cut little wedges along the curves, and turn right side out. Repeat for the second ear.

3 Lightly transfer the face markings onto the right side of both front body pieces and embroider the mouth in pink backstitch. Cut out small felt circles for the eyes—a hole punch is ideal for this job—and fix them to the heads with glue. Following the manufacturer's instructions, back a piece of pink felt large enough for the belly and inner ear pieces with fusible bonding web. Place the belly template on the felt, draw around it twice, and cut out. Appliqué the belly pieces to the body (see page 105).

5 To make the hands and feet, place the template on pink felt, draw around it four times, and cut out. Lay the finished front body sections right side up on your work surface. Place the hands and ears in position on top, aligning the raw edges and matching up the balance marks. Secure with a few machine stitches.

6 With right sides together and aligning the raw edges, lay the back body sections on top of the front sections. Pin, baste (tack), and machine stitch together. Notch the seam allowance.

7 With right sides together and aligning the raw edges, lay the right body section on top of the left body section. Pin, baste (tack), and machine stitch all the way around, apart from the straight lower edges. Leave a gap in the stitching at the back seam of the body wide enough to turn the body right side out. Trim the seam allowance to ¼ in. (5 mm) and cut out little wedges all the way around the curved edges.

8 From the remaining pink felt, cut a ⅜ x 12-in. (1 x 30-cm) strip for the tail. Place the tail and the two feet cut in Step 5 in position and secure with machine stitches. Machine stitch all the way along the bottom, ⅜ in. (1 cm) in from the bottom edge, and make small snips along the edge; this will make it easier to ease the straight edge around the curved edge of the base.

9 With right sides together, pin, baste (tack), and carefully machine stitch the base to the body of the mouse, ensuring all balance marks match and the feet and tail are neatly tucked inside. Trim all seam allowances to ¼ in. (5 mm) and cut notches around the curved edges.

10 Turn the mouse right side out, stuff with hollow fiber filling, and tuck inside the exposed seam allowance, neatly slipstitching the opening closed, using the pre-stitched lines as a guide.

11 To make the whiskers, thread a needle with stranded black embroidery floss (cotton), using all six strands. Tie a knot about 1½ in. (4 cm) from the end, then take the needle all the way through the snout. Tie another knot as close to the snout as possible, then cut the floss (cotton) so that the whiskers are the same length on both sides. Repeat three more times.

ELSA THE ELEPHANT

Every child should have a toy elephant; without doubt, they are the cutest creatures in the nursery—and extra special when made in pretty pastoral patchwork, like Elsa. Before cutting the pattern pieces in fabric, lay out the assorted pre-cut squares on your work surface and move them around until you have a pleasing arrangement. Once you have decided on the position of each pattern piece, label it. I assure you, you will thank me when it comes to the sewing stage!

YOU WILL NEED

- Pattern pieces D1–D9 and template D1 from the pull-out sheet
- Two 9½ x 10½-in. (24 x 26-cm) pieces of cotton fabric in contrasting floral prints for head
- Twelve 8 x 8-in. (20 x 20-cm) pieces of cotton fabric in contrasting floral prints for body and underbelly
- Four 6½ x 7-in. (16 x 18-cm) pieces of cotton fabric in contrasting floral prints for ears
- 8 x 9½ in. (20 x 24 cm) floral print cotton for feet bases
- Pink and turquoise stranded embroidery floss (cotton) for eyes and mouth
- White and turquoise felt scraps for eyes
- Fusible bonding web
- 6-in. (15-cm) length of pale blue felted wool knit cord for tail
- Hollow fiber filling

Other stuff

- Sewing machine
- Needle and matching sewing threads

- Take ⅜-in. (1-cm) seam allowances throughout unless otherwise stated.

1 Place the two large squares of fabric for the head wrong sides together, pin the head paper pattern on top, and cut out. For the patchwork body, take the twelve medium squares and divide them into six sets of two each, wrong sides together. Pin upper and lower body patterns 1 through 4 to the appropriate fabric set and cut out. For the underbelly, pin patterns 5 and 6 to the remaining fabric sets and cut out.

2 Remove the paper patterns, separate all the fabric shapes, and place them right side up on your work surface in their correct position, together with the elephant heads. You should have a complete left side (with its corresponding underbelly) and its mirror image, a right side and underbelly. Before you start sewing all the pieces together, make sure you are happy with the arrangement and that fabric shapes of the same pattern are not lying next to each other. If this is the case, re-cut the piece in a contrasting fabric. It's also a good idea to label each piece of fabric to facilitate sewing.

3

Starting with the left-hand side, pin, baste (tack), and machine stitch body part 1 to part 2, and part 3 to part 4. Then stitch the upper body (1, 2) to the lower part (3, 4). Press open the seam allowances as you go. Repeat for the right-hand side of the elephant. Put to one side.

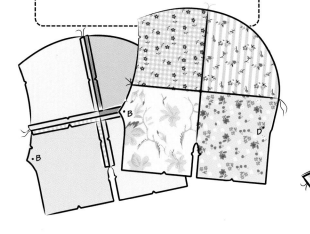

4

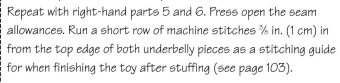

To construct the underbelly, pin, baste (tack), and machine stitch left-hand part 5 to left-hand part 6. Repeat with right-hand parts 5 and 6. Press open the seam allowances. Run a short row of machine stitches ⅜ in. (1 cm) in from the top edge of both underbelly pieces as a stitching guide for when finishing the toy after stuffing (see page 103).

5

With right sides together and aligning the raw edges, lay the right underbelly section on top of the left. Pin, baste (tack), and machine stitch along the curved edge, leaving a gap on either side of the stitching guideline that you made in the previous step so that you can turn the body right side out at a later stage. Put to one side.

6

Lightly transfer the face markings onto the right side of both head pieces. Stitch the mouth with small, close zigzag machine stitches. Following the manufacturer's instructions, back the felt with fusible bonding web. Place the eye templates on the felt, draw around each one twice, and cut out. Appliqué in place (see page 105) and put to one side.

7 Cut one ear from each of the four small fabric squares. Place them together in pairs, with right sides together and aligning the raw edges. Pin, baste (tack), and machine stitch around the curved edge only of both ears. Trim the seam allowance to ¼ in. (5 mm), cut out little wedges all the way around the curve, and turn the ears right side out.

8

Fold the ears along the foldline as indicated on the pattern piece and secure with machine stitches. Snip into the seam allowance, because this will make it easier to align the ears in the next step.

9

Lay the embellished head sections right side up on your work surface. Place the folded ears on top, aligning the raw edges, and attach with machine stitches.

10 With right sides together and matching the balance marks, pin the left head to the left body section. Baste (tack), and machine stitch together (see page 101). Cut out little wedges around the curved seams and press open. Repeat for the right-hand side of the elephant.

11

Lay the left side of the elephant on your work surface with the right side of the fabric facing up. Open out the underbelly and lay it on top, with underbelly part 5 facing body part 3 and underbelly part 6 facing body part 4. Align the raw edges and ensure the right underbelly section is clear of the fabric layers about to be stitched together. Match up points A and B, and carefully machine stitch from these points to the bottom edge of the front leg. Match up points C and D, and machine stitch from these points to the bottom edge of the back leg. Pin, baste (tack), and machine stitch the inside leg.

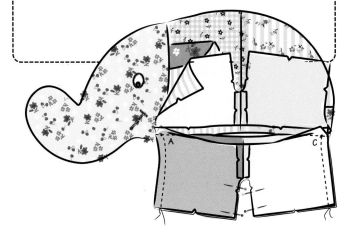

12 Lay the elephant's right side on your work surface with the right side of the fabric facing you. Repeat Step 11 to attach the right side of the elephant's underbelly, remembering to carefully match up and start sewing from points A and B and C and D.

13

Lay the elephant flat on your work surface. The two underbelly sections should now be correctly attached and sandwiched between the outer layers (left and right sides) of the elephant's body. Pin the unstitched edges together, all around the elephant—from points C and D, along the elephant's back, around the head and trunk, to points A and B, remembering to place the knitted cord tail in the correct position before pinning the seam. Baste (tack) and machine stitch, trim the seam allowances to ¼ in. (5 mm), and cut out little wedges around the curved edges.

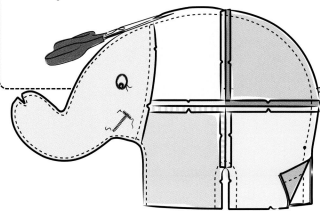

14

Pin the foot base pattern to the fabric and cut out four pieces. Before attaching them, stitch all the way along the bottom of each leg, ⅜ in. (1 cm) in from the bottom edge, and make small snips along the edges; this will make it easier to ease the straight edge of the legs around the curved edge of the foot bases. With right sides together, pin, baste (tack), and carefully machine stitch one base to each leg, ensuring all balance marks and ends of seams match.
Trim the seam allowances to ¼ in. (5 mm).

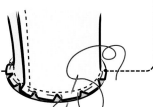

15

Turn the elephant right side out. Starting with the trunk, stuff with hollow fiber filling, making sure the toy is tightly packed in order to maintain its shape. Once the toy is completely filled, close the opening in the underbelly with slipstitching.

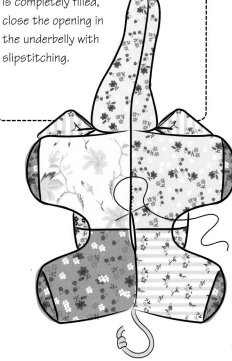

SIDNEY THE STORK

Myth and legend identify the stork as the maintainer of welfare and bringer of children—so what better gift to make for a new mom and her baby? This charming, slightly comical creature can be tied to the side of a nursery crib, and a little bag of dried lavender added to the stuffing will make the toy an even sweeter keepsake. The padded wings are a little tricky to make, but they are well worth the effort as they're so cute.

YOU WILL NEED
- Patterns E1–E2 and templates E1–E3 from the pull-out sheet
- 12 x 20 in. (30 x 50 cm) floral print fabric for body and wings
- Two 2 x 12-in. (5 x 30-cm) pieces of striped fabric for legs
- 3 x 9 in. (7 x 22 cm) plain fabric for beak
- Scraps of felt for eyes and feet
- Fusible bonding web
- 14 in. (35 cm) length of cotton tape
- 1 yd (100 cm) ribbon, ¼ in. (5 mm) wide
- Blue stranded embroidery floss (cotton)
- Hollow fiber filling

Other stuff
- Sewing machine
- Needle and matching sewing threads

- Take ⅜-in. (1-cm) seam allowances throughout unless otherwise stated.

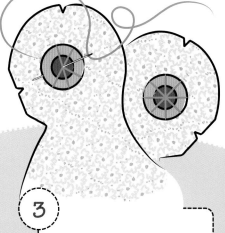

1 Fold the body and beak fabrics in half, pin the patterns on top, and cut out. Remember to transfer all markings from the paper patterns to the fabric. Remove the paper patterns.

2 Following the manufacturer's instructions, back the felt scraps for the eyes with fusible bonding web. Draw around the appliqué templates for the eyes on the paper side of the bonding web twice, and cut out.

3 Lay both body sections right side up on your work surface. Place the large circle eyes in position and fix with a hot iron (see page 105). Lay the smaller circles on top and repeat. Work a single star stitch (see page 104) across each eye.

4

With right sides together, pin, baste (tack), and machine stitch the beaks to the body sections. Press the seam allowances toward the tip of the beak.

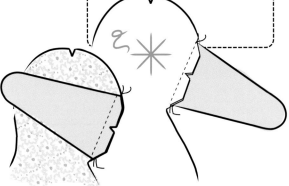

5 Fold the striped fabric for the legs in half lengthwise, right sides together, sandwiching a length of cotton tape that is longer than the strip in between the layers. Machine stitch across one short end and along the whole length of each strip, taking care not to catch the tape in the stitching. Pull the cotton tape and turn the strips right side out. Cut off the closed ends of the strips and roll with your fingers until the seams are positioned on one side.

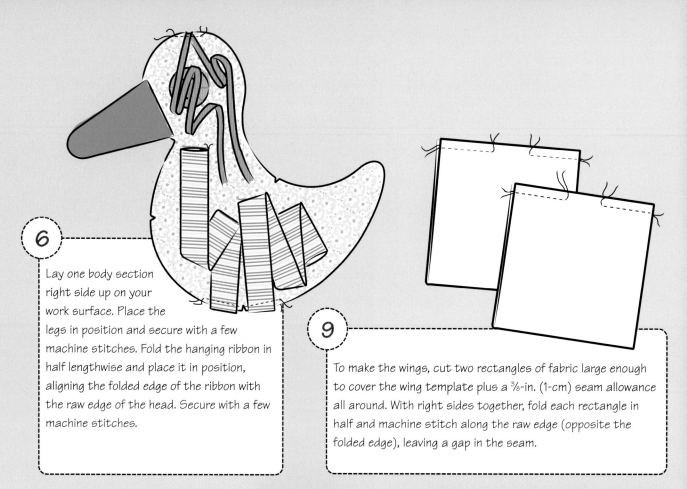

6 Lay one body section right side up on your work surface. Place the legs in position and secure with a few machine stitches. Fold the hanging ribbon in half lengthwise and place it in position, aligning the folded edge of the ribbon with the raw edge of the head. Secure with a few machine stitches.

9 To make the wings, cut two rectangles of fabric large enough to cover the wing template plus a ⅜-in. (1-cm) seam allowance all around. With right sides together, fold each rectangle in half and machine stitch along the raw edge (opposite the folded edge), leaving a gap in the seam.

7 With right sides together, aligning the raw edges and making sure that the legs and hanging ribbon are neatly tucked inside, lay the back body section on top of the front section. Pin, baste (tack), and machine stitch all around, leaving a gap in the base wide enough to turn the stork right side out. Trim the seam allowance to ¼ in. (5 mm) and cut little notches around all the curved edges.

8 Turn the stork right side out and stuff the body with hollow fiber filling. Tuck in the seam allowance around the opening and neatly slipstitch the opening closed (see page 103 Step 3).

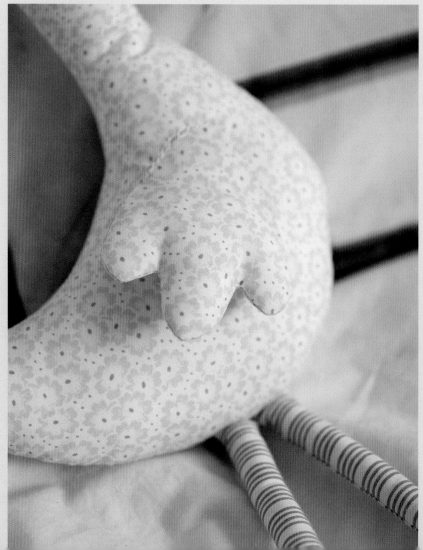

10

Fold the fabric so that the seam is in the center and press the seam allowances to either side. Lay the wing template on the first piece of fabric, draw around it, and carefully machine stitch along the drawn line. Cut out the wing, cutting ¼ in. (5 mm) beyond the stitching line, and cut notches in the seam allowance all around the curves. Turn the wing right side out, stuff with hollow fiber filling, and slipstitch the opening closed. Repeat to make the second wing.

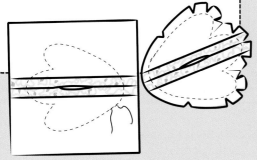

11

Place one wing on each side of the body and hand stitch it in place, stitching around the top curve only.

12 Stuff the legs with hollow fiber filling and secure the ends with machine stitches.

13

Place the template for the foot on the felt and draw around it four times. Cut out all the pieces. Lay one foot on top of another and zigzag stitch all the way around, leaving the top end open. Insert the leg into the opening and close with a row of zigzag stitches. Repeat for the other foot.

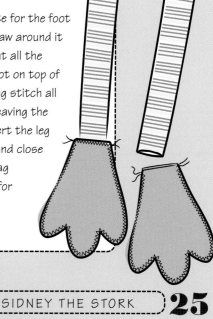

2. Nursery novelties

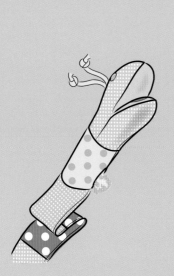

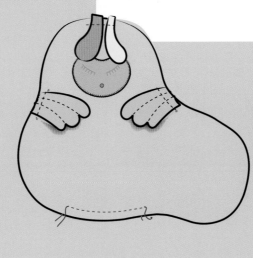

CASPER THE COMFORTER

Fashioned in felt and knitted fleece, this delectable soft toy doubles as a pillow. Made *en masse* and stitched together in a row, this design will make a fun "bumper" for a crib. Increase the comfort factor by adding a small muslin bag of calming dried lavender to the stuffing. Alternatively, turn it into a rattle by placing a bell inside a small cotton bag that has been attached securely to the inside seam by cotton tape.

YOU WILL NEED

- Pattern F1 and templates F1–F4 from the pull-out sheet
- 10½ x 24 in. (26 x 60 cm) turquoise knitted fleece for body
- 2½ x 3½ in. (6 x 8 cm) pink felt for face
- Scraps of double-thickness felt for antennae
- Two 3 x 5½-in. (7 x 14-cm) pieces of plain cotton fabric for wings
- Turquoise embroidery floss (cotton) for eyelashes
- Scrap of pink felt for mouth
- 4 x 8 in. (10 x 20 cm) fusible bonding web
- Hollow fiber filling

Other stuff

- Sewing machine
- Needle and matching sewing threads
- Glue
- Take ⅜-in. (1-cm) seam allowances throughout unless otherwise stated.

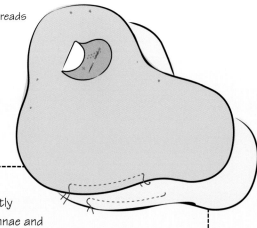

1 Fold the body fabric in half, pin the pattern on top, and cut out two pieces. Transfer the balance marks from the paper pattern to the fabric. Remove the paper pattern.

2 Using a pencil, lightly transfer the antennae and wing markings onto the right side of one of the body pieces. Run a short row of machine stitches ⅜ in. (1 cm) in from the bottom edge of both body pieces as a guide for when finishing the toy after stuffing (see page 103). Back the pink felt for the face with fusible bonding web. Place the face template on the felt, draw around it, and cut out. Appliqué (see page 105) the face to the body.

3

Embroider the eyelashes in turquoise backstitch (see page 104). Cut out a small circle of felt for the mouth (a hole punch is ideal for this) and glue it to the face.

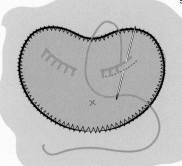

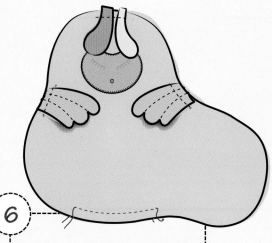

4 Lay the antennae templates on the scraps of double-thickness felt, draw around them, cut out, and put to one side.

6

Lay the body piece with the appliquéd face right side up on your work surface. Place the antennae and wings in position and secure with a few machine stitches.

5

For each wing, cut a 3 x 5½-in. (7 x 14-cm) rectangle of fabric to cover the wing template plus a seam allowance. With right sides together, fold the material in half. Lay the wing template on the material (with all straight edges aligned), draw around it, and carefully machine stitch along the drawn line. Cut out the wing, cutting ¼ in. (5 mm) beyond the stitching line, and cut notches in the seam allowance all around the curves. Turn the wing right side out, stitch the channel lines, and carefully stuff the channels with hollow fiber filling, using tweezers. To secure the opening, sink stitches through all layers, ⅝ in. (1.5 cm) in from the straight raw edge.

7 With right sides together, aligning the raw edges and ensuring the wings and antennae are neatly tucked inside, lay the back body section on top of the front section. Pin, baste (tack), and machine stitch all around, leaving a gap in the base wide enough to turn the toy right side out. Trim the seam allowance to ¼ in. (5 mm) and cut out little wedges around the curved edges.

8 Turn the body right side out and stuff with hollow fiber filling. Tuck in the seam allowance around the opening and neatly slipstitch the opening closed (see page 103 Step 3), using the pre-stitched lines as a guide.

ONDINE THE MERMAID

This little mermaid will warm the cockles of your heart! A pair of scallop shells, a curving fishtail in shimmering lamé, and a flowing mane of ribbon tendrils will captivate every little girl—and every little boy, for that matter. (Hey, why should girls have all the fun?!) This nautical nymph is quick and easy to make, but take special care when embroidering the face and stuffing the fishtail.

YOU WILL NEED

- Pattern pieces G1–G2 and templates G1–G2 from the pull-out sheet
- 12 x 24 in. (30 x 60 cm) pale blue cotton fabric for body
- 9 x 21½ in. (22 x 54 cm) blue lamé for fishtail and scallop shells
- Lilac and turquoise stranded embroidery floss (cotton) for features
- Fusible bonding web
- White and lilac felt scraps for eyes

- Hollow fiber filling
- 24-in. (60-cm) lengths of jumbo rickrack and ¼-in. ½-in., and ⅝-in. (5 mm, 10 mm, and 15 mm) ribbon in tonal colors

Other stuff
- Sewing machine
- Needle and matching sewing threads

- Take ⅜-in. (1-cm) seam allowances throughout unless otherwise stated.

1 Pin the body pattern to the folded cotton and the fishtail pattern to the folded lamé. Cut out two pieces of each. Remove the paper patterns.

2 Run a short row of machine stitches ⅜ in. (1 cm) in from the one side of both fishtail pieces as a guide for when finishing the toy after stuffing (see page 103).

3 Lightly transfer the face markings onto the right side of one body piece and embroider the nose with a turquoise straight stitch and the mouth in lilac backstitch (see page 104). Cut out circles and ovals of white and lilac felt for the eyes, and appliqué them in place (see page 105). Add three stitches in white embroidery thread to each pupil to make them twinkle and three straight stitches in turquoise to create eyelashes. Cut a 4 x 3-in. (10 x 8-cm) piece of lamé and back it with fusible bonding web. Place the scallop shell template on top, draw around it twice, and cut out. Appliqué the shells to the upper torso. Embroider a belly button with a French knot.

4

With right sides together, pin, baste (tack), and machine stitch the body pieces to the fishtails.

5 With right sides together and aligning the raw edges, pin, baste (tack), and machine stitch all around, leaving a gap in the side of the fishtail wide enough to turn the toy right side out. Carefully trim the seam allowance to ¼ in. (5 mm) and cut out little wedges around the curved edges.

6 Turn the mermaid right side out and stuff with hollow fiber filling. Tuck in the exposed seam allowance, and neatly slipstitch the opening closed, using the pre-stitched lines as a guide.

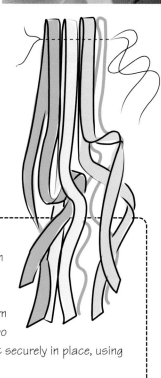

7

To make the tendril hair, take lengths of ribbon folded in half and lay them side by side to create a strip of fringing. Carefully machine stitch through the ribbons ¾ in. (2 cm) in from the folds. Lay a 24-in. (60-cm) length of jumbo rickrack over this fringe of ribbon and stitch it securely in place, using the previous line of stitches as a guide.

8

Attach the fringe to the head with glue or hand stitches, following the seamline of the head.

EGBERT THE EGGHEAD

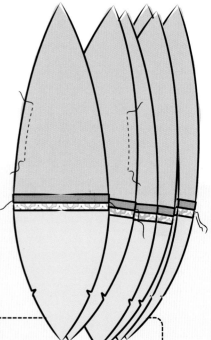

With his orange quiff and purple boots, Egbert is a really cool dude! He is inspired by "Humpty," a green-velvet egg-shaped toy on the British children's TV show *Play School*. Stuff the toy well to maintain its distinctive egg shape—and if you find the stuffed nose too fiddly to make, an appliquéd felt circle in a contrasting color is an ideal alternative.

YOU WILL NEED

- Pattern pieces H1–H6 and templates H1–H3 from the pull-out sheet
- 17½ x 24 in. (44 x 60 cm) plain cotton fabric for the head, nose, and hands
- 17½ x 24 in. (44 x 60 cm) printed cotton fabric for the body, arms, and legs
- 9½ x 10½ in. (24 x 26 cm) contrasting plain cotton fabric for the boots
- Brown, white, pink, and green felt scraps for features and buttons
- Seven 8½-in. (21-cm) lengths of orange felted wool knit cord for hair
- Deep pink stranded embroidery floss (cotton)
- Hollow fiber filling

Other stuff
- Sewing machine
- Needle and matching sewing threads
- Glue

- Take ⅜-in. (1-cm) seam allowances throughout unless otherwise stated.

1 Pin the head pattern to the plain cotton and cut out six pieces. From the remnants of the plain cotton, using the hand pattern and the nose template, cut four hands and a circle for the nose. Pin the body, arm, and leg patterns to the printed cotton and cut out six body pieces, four arms, and four legs. Pin the boot pattern to the contrasting plain cotton and cut out four boot pieces.

2 With right sides together and aligning the straight edges, machine stitch each head piece to a body piece to create six long segments. Press open the seams. Take two of the segments and, in the head areas, run a short row of machine stitches ⅜ in. (1 cm) in from two sides that will eventually be joined together. These rows of stitches will be matched up at a later stage and used as a guide for when finishing the toy after stuffing (see page 103).

3 With right sides together and aligning the straight edges, machine stitch the legs to the boots. Press open the seams.

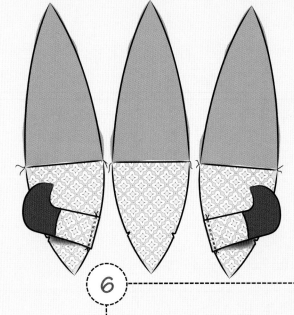

4

With right sides together and aligning the raw edges, lay a back leg on top of a front leg. Pin, baste (tack), and machine stitch all the way around, leaving a gap in the stitching at the back seam wide enough to push in fiber stuffing. Trim the seam allowance to ¼ in. (5 mm), cut out little wedges along the curved edge, and turn the leg right side out. Repeat for the other leg. Put both legs to one side.

6

To make the front part of the toy, lay three long segments right side up in a line on your work surface. Place the legs in position on the inside edge of the two outer segments and secure with machine stitches.

5 Repeat Steps 3 and 4 for the arms, but do not leave a gap in the back seam. Stuff the arms with hollow fiber filling and close the openings with machine stitches ⅜ in. (1 cm) in from the raw edge.

7 With right sides together and aligning the inner raw edges, lay the left segment on top of the middle segment; pin, baste (tack), and machine stitch all the way along the curve. Cut out little wedges all the way along the edge and press open the seam. Repeat the process for the right segment, leaving a gap in the stitching wide enough to turn the toy right side out in Step 11.

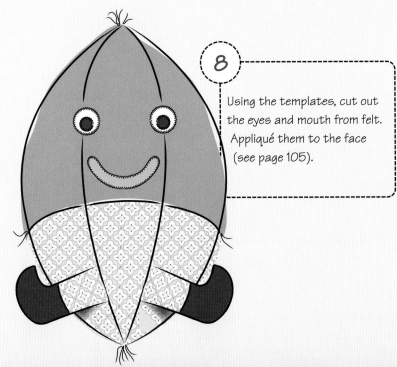

8

Using the templates, cut out the eyes and mouth from felt. Appliqué them to the face (see page 105).

9

To make a looped fringe, take seven 8½-in. (21-cm) strands of felted wool knit cord, fold them in half, lay them side by side at the center top of the head, and machine stitch in place.

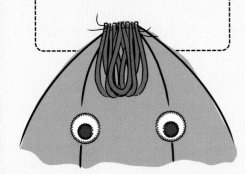

11

With right sides together, aligning the raw edges and matching up the converging seams at top and bottom, place the front section inside the back section. Pin, baste (tack), and machine stitch all the way around, ensuring the "waist" seams match up and the feet and arms are neatly tucked inside the two layers. Cut notches all the way around the curved edges and turn the toy right side out, carefully pulling it through the opening made in Step 7.

10

To make the back part of the toy repeat Steps 6 and 7, remembering to attach the arms to the outside edges of the left and right segments, just below the central "waist" seam.

12 First, stuff the legs with hollow fiber filling and close the openings with slipstitching. Next, stuff the body cavity and tuck inside the exposed seam allowance, neatly slipstitching the opening closed, using the pre-stitched lines as a guide (see page 103).

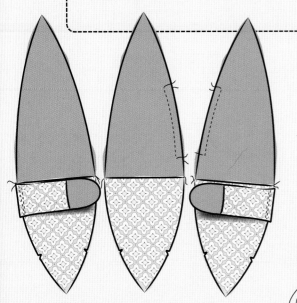

13

To make the nose, gather the outer edge of the circle of fabric by hand or machine (see page 102) to form a little pouch bag. Stuff the cavity with hollow fiber filling and pull the threads tight to close the opening. Secure the gathers with hand stitches. Stick the nose to the face with fabric glue.

14 Sew "buttons" made from a double thickness of green felt to the front of Egbert's body.

PERRY THE PONY

This noble little pony has an indefinable spark of magic about him. With his naïve shape, bold color, and rhythmic pattern, he oozes an abundance of childlike charm. A flamboyant mane and tail in vibrant green yarn add to his character. Take extra care when stuffing the head and legs to achieve a nice shape.

YOU WILL NEED

- Template 11 from the pull-out sheet
- 10½ x 21½ in. (26 x 54 cm) floral print fabric for pony
- One 2-oz (50-g) ball pure wool light worsted (double knitting) yarn, for mane and ponytail
- Hollow fiber filling

Other stuff

- Sewing machine
- Needle and matching sewing threads

1 Fold the fabric for the pony in half, right sides together. Place the template for the pony on the fabric and draw around it.

2 Smooth the fabric, still folded in half, so that there are no wrinkles, then pin the layers together, and carefully machine stitch along the drawn line, leaving a gap below the tail to turn the toy right side out. Remove the pins.

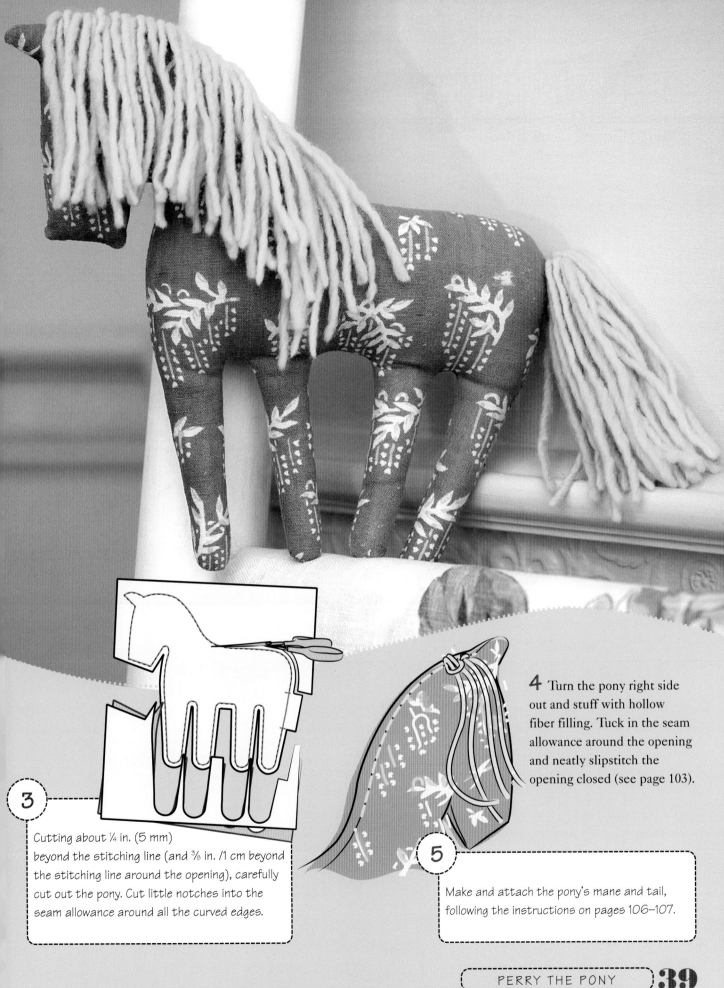

3

Cutting about ¼ in. (5 mm) beyond the stitching line (and ⅜ in. /1 cm beyond the stitching line around the opening), carefully cut out the pony. Cut little notches into the seam allowance around all the curved edges.

4 Turn the pony right side out and stuff with hollow fiber filling. Tuck in the seam allowance around the opening and neatly slipstitch the opening closed (see page 103).

5

Make and attach the pony's mane and tail, following the instructions on pages 106–107.

WILBUR THE GLOW-WORM

Unlike ordinary brown and boring worms, Wilbur is distinctively dapper in "Day-Glo" colors. And he's a happy chap, too—that's why he has such a huge grin on his face. He's quite content to sit in the sun, drape himself over a chair, twist his way around the ladder of a bunk bed, or curve around a crib for a highly individual "bumper." With his eye-popping colors and playful patterns, he'll have little ones in stitches—and they in turn can tie him in knots.

YOU WILL NEED

- Pattern pieces J1–J5 and templates J1–J2 from the pull-out sheet
- 16 x 16 in. (40 x 40 cm) spotted cotton fabric for the head and tail
- Fourteen 7 x 11-in. (18 x 27-cm) pieces of spotted cotton fabric in assorted contrast/tonal colors for the body
- 4 x 8 in. (10 x 20 cm) pale pink cotton fabric for the mouth
- 2¾ x 2¾ in. (7 x 7 cm) hot pink cotton fabric for the tongue
- Fusible bonding web

- Spotted cotton fabric scraps for eyes
- Two x 4¾-in. (12-cm) lengths of pale blue felted wool knit cord for antennae
- Hollow fiber filling

Other stuff

- Sewing machine
- Needle and matching sewing threads

- Take ⅜-in. (1-cm) seam allowances throughout unless otherwise stated.

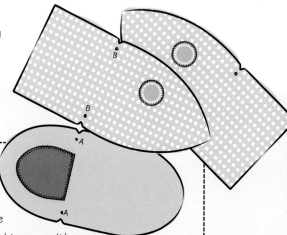

1 Pin the head and tail patterns to the spotted fabric. Cut out two heads and two tails. Remove the paper patterns. Using a pencil, lightly transfer the stitching points onto the wrong sides of the pieces. Pin the mouth pattern to the pale pink fabric and cut out one piece

2 Following the manufacturer's instructions, back the fabrics for the eye and tongue with fusible bonding web. Place the eye and tongue templates on the fabrics. Draw around the eye template twice and around the tongue once, and cut out. Appliqué (see page 105) the eyes to the upper head and the tongue to the mouth interior.

3 With right sides together and aligning the raw edges, pin, baste (tack), and machine stitch the two upper head pieces together along the top curved edge, remembering to place the antennae in the dot position before joining the seam. Trim the seam allowance to ¼ in. (5 mm) and cut out little wedges around the curved edge.

5 With right sides together and aligning the raw edges, pin, baste (tack), and machine stitch the two lower jaw pieces together along the bottom curved edge. Trim the seam allowance to ¼ in. (5 mm) and cut out little wedges around the curved edge.

4 With right sides together, aligning the raw edges, and matching up points A and B, pin, baste (tack), and machine stitch the mouth to the upper head. Make small snips along the lower raw edges of the upper head in order to make it easier to ease the fabric around the curved edge of the mouth.

6 With right sides together, aligning the raw edges, and matching up points A and C, pin, baste (tack), and machine stitch the mouth interior to the lower jaw. Make small snips along the lower raw edges of the lower jaw in order to make it easier to ease the fabric around the curved edge of the mouth.

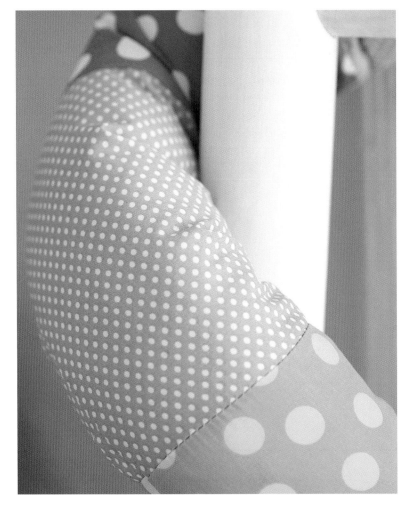

7 Lay the head flat on your work surface. Pin the open left- and right-hand sides together, ensuring points A, B, and C match up. Baste (tack) and then carefully machine stitch the open sides together, from the matching-up points to the open end on the head. Trim all seam allowances to ¼ in. (5 mm) and put to one side.

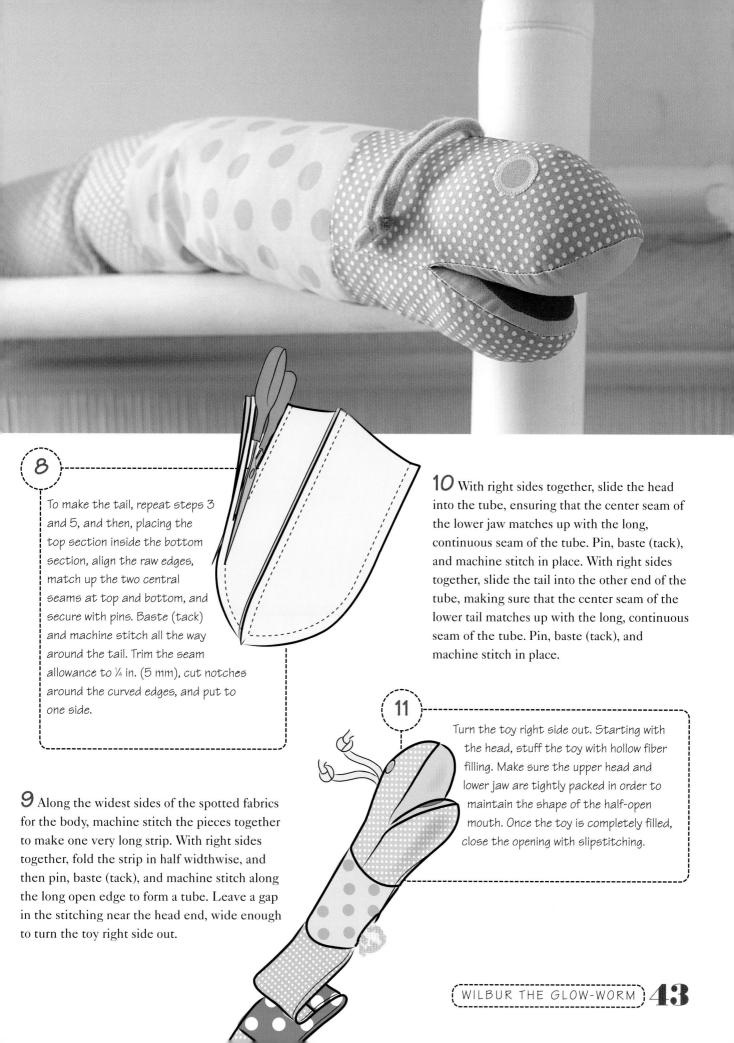

8 To make the tail, repeat steps 3 and 5, and then, placing the top section inside the bottom section, align the raw edges, match up the two central seams at top and bottom, and secure with pins. Baste (tack) and machine stitch all the way around the tail. Trim the seam allowance to ¼ in. (5 mm), cut notches around the curved edges, and put to one side.

9 Along the widest sides of the spotted fabrics for the body, machine stitch the pieces together to make one very long strip. With right sides together, fold the strip in half widthwise, and then pin, baste (tack), and machine stitch along the long open edge to form a tube. Leave a gap in the stitching near the head end, wide enough to turn the toy right side out.

10 With right sides together, slide the head into the tube, ensuring that the center seam of the lower jaw matches up with the long, continuous seam of the tube. Pin, baste (tack), and machine stitch in place. With right sides together, slide the tail into the other end of the tube, making sure that the center seam of the lower tail matches up with the long, continuous seam of the tube. Pin, baste (tack), and machine stitch in place.

11 Turn the toy right side out. Starting with the head, stuff the toy with hollow fiber filling. Make sure the upper head and lower jaw are tightly packed in order to maintain the shape of the half-open mouth. Once the toy is completely filled, close the opening with slipstitching.

3. Activity toys

BOO!

Half hiding under his polo-neck sweater, Boo! is a shy little fellow. He's rather odd, too, and has a very strange habit of multiplying—probably because he's so easy to make. Boo! and his multiple personalities have been made in cosy knitted fleece—perfect for little ones to cuddle up to. If you prefer, you could use woven cotton fabrics in plain colors, stripes, spots, or florals.

YOU WILL NEED

- Patterns K1–K2 from the pull-out sheet
- Three 3¾ x 4¾-in. (9 x 12-cm) pieces of fleece in white, pale pink, and brown for the heads
- Three 9 x 16-in. (22 x 40-cm) pieces of fleece in lilac, yellow, and fuchsia for the bodies

- Three small ready-made pompoms in blue, yellow, and red
- Ivory, pink, brown, and blue stranded embroidery floss (cotton)
- Hollow fiber filling

Other stuff
- Sewing machine
- Needle and matching sewing threads
- Glue

- Take ⅜-in. (1-cm) seam allowances throughout unless otherwise stated.

1 Fold the body and head fabrics in half, pin the patterns on top, and cut out two of each. Transfer all markings from the patterns to the fabric. Remove the paper patterns.

2

Lightly transfer the face markings onto the right side of one of the head pieces. Embroider the eyes and nose, using large French knots (see page 104).

4

With right sides together and aligning the raw edges, pin, baste (tack), and machine stitch the heads to the bodies. Press open the seams.

3

Lightly transfer the arm markings onto the right side of one of the body pieces. Embroider the arms, using backstitch (see page 104). Run a short row of machine stitches ⅜ in. (1 cm) in from the bottom edge of both body pieces as a guide for when finishing the toy after stuffing (see page 103).

5

Place the front and back pieces right sides together. Machine stitch all the way around, leaving a gap at the base wide enough to turn the body right side out. Trim the seam allowance to ¼ in. (5 mm) and cut little notches into the seam allowance around all the curved edges.

6

Turn the body right side out and stuff with hollow fiber filling. Tuck in the seam allowance around the opening and neatly slipstitch the opening closed, using the pre-stitched lines as a guide (see page 103). Glue three pompoms to the top of the head.

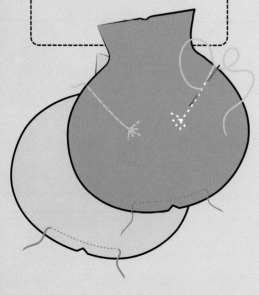
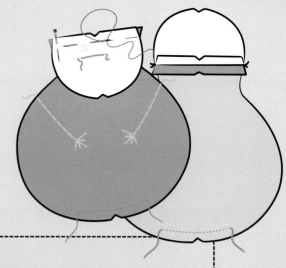

BABUSHKA BASKET

Natesha, Natasha, and Natosha are—you guessed it—Russian triplets! Soft and cuddly Matryoshka-inspired baby dolls, slumbering soundly in their cosy crib, they're so tiny that they can be wrapped up in handkerchiefs to protect them from the cruel Russian winter.

YOU WILL NEED

For the dolls

- Patterns L1–L2 and template L1 from the pull-out sheet
- Three 5½ x 10½-in. (14 x 26-cm) pieces of plain fabric for the heads
- Three 5½ x 10½-in. (14 x 26-cm) pieces of floral print fabric for the bodies
- 2½ x 5½ in. (6 x 14 cm) felt for the faces
- 2½ x 5½ in. (6 x 14 cm) fusible bonding web
- Three 9½-in. (24-cm lengths of jumbo rickrack
- Stranded embroidery floss (cotton) for eyes and noses
- Floral trim
- Hollow fiber filling

For the crib

- 9 x 10½ in. (22 x 26 cm) felt for the base
- 3½ x 36 in. (8 x 90 cm) felt for the sides
- 38 in. (95 cm) bias binding, 1 in. (2.5 cm) wide

For the mattress pad

- Two 10½ x 12-in. (26 x 30-cm) pieces of striped fabric
- Stranded embroidery floss (cotton)
- Hollow fiber filling

For the handkerchief "blankets"

- Three 9½-in. (24-cm) squares of floral fabric
- Three 9-in. (22-cm) lengths of broderie anglaise trim

Other stuff

- Sewing machine
- Needle and matching sewing threads
- Take ⅜-in. (1-cm) seam allowances throughout unless otherwise stated.

1 For each doll, pin the head pattern to the plain fabric and cut out twice. Pin the body pattern to the print fabric and cut out twice. Remove the paper patterns.

2 Following the manufacturer's instructions, back the felt scrap for the face with fusible bonding web. Draw around the face template on the paper side of the bonding web and cut out. Appliqué (see page 105) the face to the head.

3 To make the "sleepy" eyes and "rosebud" mouth, transfer the facial features from the pattern onto the felt with a pencil (see page 100). Embroider the eyes in backstitch and the mouth with a French knot (see page 104).

4

With right sides together, pin the front head piece to the front body piece. Baste (tack) and machine stitch together. Press open the seam. Repeat with the back head and body pieces.

5

Stitch a 4¾-in. (12-cm) length of jumbo rickrack over the seam between the front head and body. Repeat on the back.

6 With right sides together, aligning the raw edges, pin and baste (tack) the front and back of the doll together. Machine stitch all around, leaving a gap at the bottom to turn the doll right side out. Trim the seam allowance to ¼ in. (5 mm), cut off the right-angled corners, and cut notches around the curved edges.

7 Turn the doll right side out. Stuff with hollow fiber filling. Tuck in the seam allowance around the opening and neatly slipstitch the opening closed (see page 103). Stitch a fabric daisy to the doll's head.

8 To make the crib, stitch together the two short ends of the long felt strip. Press the seam open and secure the seam edges with zig-zag stitches. Make a pair of handles using two 6-in. (15-cm) lengths of binding and attach to the sides of the strip. Pin, baste (tack), and machine stitch the bias binding in place all along the top edge of the strip (see page 106), with the handles centered on what will be the short sides of the crib, making sure that the raw edges of the handles are caught underneath the binding.

9 With right sides facing each other and all edges aligned, carefully pin and baste (tack) the bottom edge of the strip to the felt rectangle. Machine stitch in place, snipping the lower edge of the strip as you turn the corners. Trim the seam allowance to ¼ in. (5 mm), cut off the right-angled corners, and turn right side out.

10 With right sides together, aligning the raw edges, pin and baste (tack) the two mattress pieces together. Machine stitch all around, leaving a gap at one short end to turn the mattress right side out. Trim off the right-angled corners, turn right side out, and press the seamed edges. Lightly stuff the mattress. Tuck in the seam allowance around the opening, and slipstitch the opening closed.

11 Stitch French knots (see page 104) across the mattress at regular intervals, stitching through all thicknesses. Double hem (by ¼ in./5 mm and then by another ¼ in./5 mm) the edges of the three squares of printed cotton to make handkerchief "blankets." Decorate the top edge of each blanket with a length of broderie anglaise in a coordinating color.

CALVIN THE KITTY-KAT

Calvin is a very happy kitty-cat—not surprisingly, as he's holding tightly on to his fish supper of a plump red snapper! This adorable toy and his tasty treat can help teach your child how to button-up and can also be used to explain giving and receiving through role playing.

YOU WILL NEED

For Calvin

- Patterns M1–M8 and templates M1–M5 from the pull-out sheet
- 16 x 20 in. (40 x 50 cm) wool herringbone for body, legs, and tail
- 7 x 10 in. (18 x 25 cm) claret felt for face, feet, and tail tip
- 4¾ x 7 in. (12 x 18 cm) double-thickness claret felt for arms
- 3¾ x 3¾ in. (9 x 9 cm) red felt for muzzle and button
- Scrap of black felt for eyes
- 4¾ x 6½ in. (12 x 16 cm) fusible bonding web
- White, peach, and brown stranded embroidery floss (cotton)

For Calvin's fish supper

- 7 x 9 in. (18 x 22 cm) melange linen
- 2½ x 4 in. (6 x 10 cm) plain cotton fabric for face
- 2½ x 4 in. (6 x 10 cm) fusible bonding web
- Olive and pink stranded embroidery floss (cotton)

Other stuff

- Hollow fiber filling
- Sewing machine
- Needle and matching sewing threads

- Take ⅜-in. (1-cm) seam allowances throughout unless otherwise stated.

To make Calvin

1 Pin the pattern pieces to the relevant fabrics. Cut one front and one back body, one front and one back tail, and two front arms and two back arms from the herringbone fabric. Cut one tail tip and two leg tips from claret felt. Remove all the paper patterns.

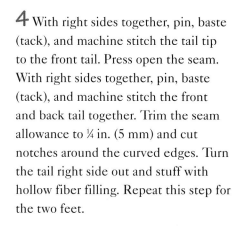

2 Lightly transfer the arm and leg markings onto the right side of one of the body pieces with chalk. Run a short row of machine stitches ⅜ in. (1 cm) in from the bottom edge of both body pieces as a guide for when finishing the toy after stuffing (see page 103). Following the manufacturer's instructions, back the claret and red felt with fusible bonding web. Place the face template onto the claret felt and the muzzle template on the red felt, draw around them, and cut out. Appliqué (see page 105) the face and muzzle to the body.

3 Embroider the nose in pink satin stitch (see page 104) and the mouth in brown backstitch (see page 104). Cut the eyes from black felt and hand stitch them to the face, using embroidery floss (cotton).

4 With right sides together, pin, baste (tack), and machine stitch the tail tip to the front tail. Press open the seam. With right sides together, pin, baste (tack), and machine stitch the front and back tail together. Trim the seam allowance to ¼ in. (5 mm) and cut notches around the curved edges. Turn the tail right side out and stuff with hollow fiber filling. Repeat this step for the two feet.

5 Cut two arms from the double-thickness claret felt and put to one side.

6 Lay the appliquéd body section right side up on your work surface. Place the arms and legs in position and secure with a few machine stitches.

7 With right sides together, aligning the raw edges and ensuring the arms and legs are neatly tucked inside, lay the back body section on top of the front section. Pin, baste (tack), and machine stitch all around, leaving a gap in the base wide enough to attach the tail and turn the toy right side out. Trim the seam allowance to ¼ in. (5mm) and cut out little wedges around the curved edges.

8 Turn the body right side out. Insert the tail into the opening and, aligning the raw edges, machine stitch the tail in place. Stuff the toy with hollow fiber filling. Tuck in the seam allowance around the opening and neatly slipstitch the opening closed (see page 103), using the pre-stitched lines as a guide. Make a "buttonhole" cut in one arm and sew a "button" made from a double thickness of red felt to the other arm.

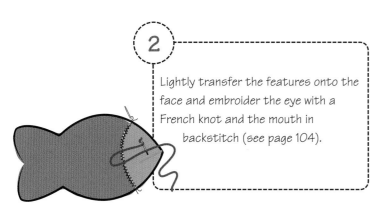

To make Calvin's fish supper

1 Fold the fish fabric in half, pin the pattern on top, and cut out. Transfer all markings from the paper pattern to the fabric. Remove the paper pattern. Back the plain cotton for the face with fusible bonding web. Draw around the face template, cut one face, and appliqué it in position (see page 105).

2 Lightly transfer the features onto the face and embroider the eye with a French knot and the mouth in backstitch (see page 104).

3 With right sides together and aligning the raw edges, pin, baste (tack), and machine stitch all around the fish, leaving a gap in the belly wide enough to turn the toy right side out. Trim the seam allowance to ¼ in. (5 mm) and cut little notches into the seam allowance around all the curved edges (see page 101).

4 Turn the body right side out and stuff with hollow fiber filling. Tuck in the seam allowance around the opening and neatly slipstitch the opening closed (see page 103).

REYNARD AND HENRIETTA

Simple in shape yet bold in design, this topsy-turvy toy will fascinate little ones and provide them with additional fun when the bedtime story-telling hour approaches. I like the idea of using wholesome, honest-to-goodness country checks to conceal and reveal these farmyard foes, but stripes, spots, or florals could work just as well. To make felt more substantial for free-standing pieces, sandwich fusible bonding web between two layers before cutting out the pattern pieces.

YOU WILL NEED
- Patterns N1–N2 and templates N1–N4 from the pull-out sheet

For Reynard the fox
- 10 x 12¾ in. (25 x 32 cm) brown felt for body
- Scrap of double-thickness brown felt for arms
- 9 x 16½ in. (22 x 42 cm) green-and-white cotton gingham for skirt
- Ivory and turquoise stranded embroidery floss (cotton) for features

For Henrietta the hen
- 8 x 11 in. (20 x 28 cm) yellow felt for body
- Scraps of double-thickness yellow, red, and orange felt for wing, comb, and beak
- 9 x 16¾ in. (22 x 42 cm) red-and-white cotton gingham for skirt
- Turquoise and orange stranded embroidery floss (cotton) for eye and wing trim
- Hollow fiber filling

Other stuff
- Sewing machine
- Needle and matching sewing threads

- Take ⅜-in. (1-cm) seam allowances throughout unless otherwise stated.

Reynard the fox

1 Pin the body pattern to the folded felt and cut out. Remember to transfer all markings from the paper pattern to the fabric. Remove the paper pattern.

2 Lightly transfer the face markings onto the head area of one of the body pieces and embroider the eye in backstitch and satin stitch, the mouth and nose in backstitch, and the whiskers in small single stitches (see page 103).

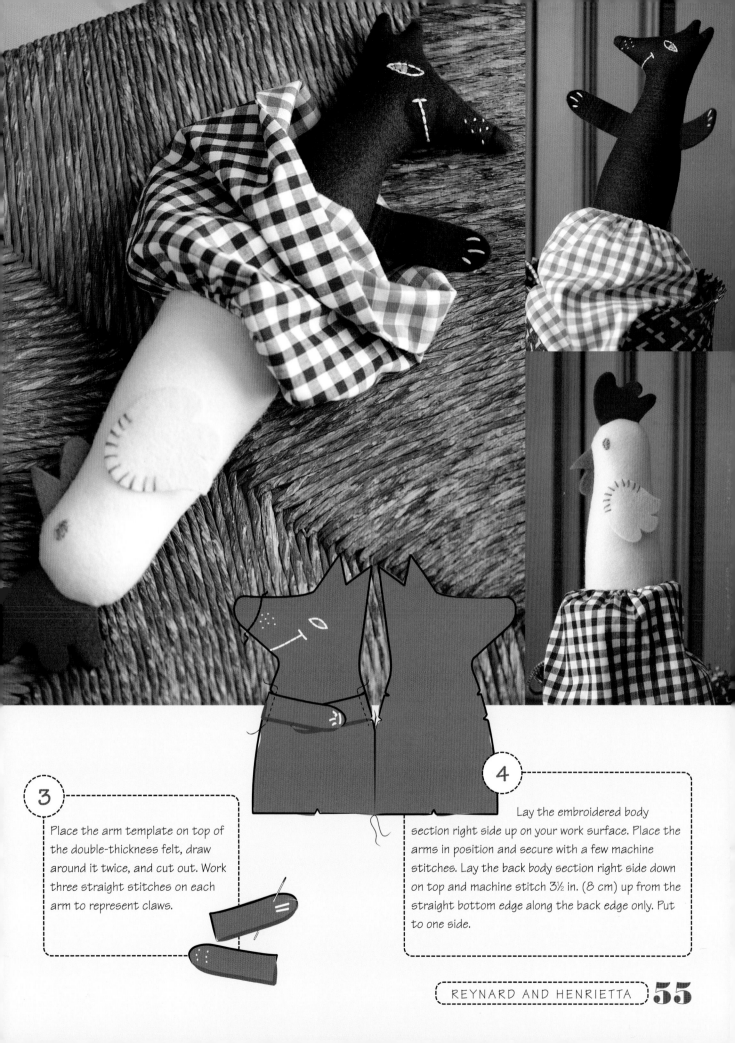

3

Place the arm template on top of the double-thickness felt, draw around it twice, and cut out. Work three straight stitches on each arm to represent claws.

4

Lay the embroidered body section right side up on your work surface. Place the arms in position and secure with a few machine stitches. Lay the back body section right side down on top and machine stitch 3½ in. (8 cm) up from the straight bottom edge along the back edge only. Put to one side.

Henrietta the hen

1 Pin the body pattern to the folded felt and cut out. Remember to transfer all markings from the paper pattern to the fabric. Remove the paper pattern. Run a short row of machine stitches ⅜ in. (1 cm) in from the back edge of both body pieces as a guide for when finishing the toy after stuffing (see page 103).

2 Lightly transfer the eye marking onto the head area of one of the body pieces. Outline the eye in turquoise backstitch, and then fill it in with satin stitch (see page 104).

3 Place the wing, comb, and beak templates on top of their respective pieces of double-thickness felt, draw around them, and cut out.

4 Lay the embroidered-eye body section right side up on your work surface. Place the comb and beak in position and secure with machine stitches. Lay the back body section right side down on top and machine stitch 3½ in. (8 cm) up from the straight bottom edge along the back edge only. Put to one side.

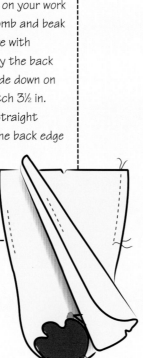

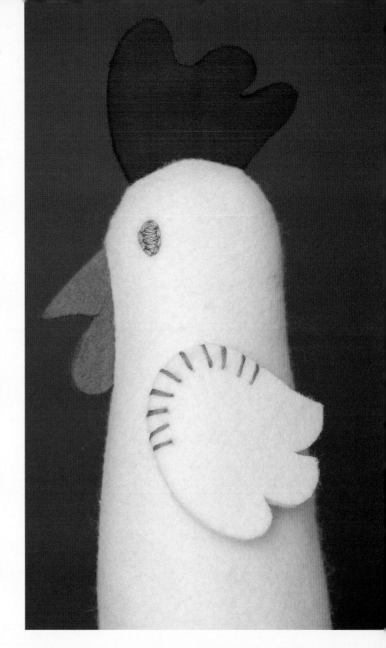

Assembling the toy

1 To make the reversible skirt, lay the two gingham panels one on top of the other with right sides together. Pin, baste (tack), and machine stitch along the hem and the two short sides, making sure both panels are flat. Turn the skirt right side out and then carefully press the layers back onto each other, ensuring you have crisp, "on-the-seam" edges.

2 Gather the top edge of the skirt panel by hand or machine to about 8 in./20 cm (see page 102). With the straight, raw edges aligned, lay the panel on top of Reynard's joined body with the green-and-white gingham side facing him, making sure that both ends of the panel fall ever-so-slightly short of the ⅜-in. (1-cm) seam allowances on the outer edges of the fox. Taking the required seam allowance, machine stitch the panel to the fox.

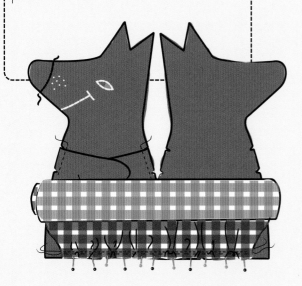

4 Roll up the skirt vertically and as tightly as possible, and fold the hen and fox back on themselves, right sides together. Aligning the raw edges, and making sure that the skirt, arms, comb, and beak are neatly tucked inside, pin, baste (tack), and machine stitch all the way around the outside edge of the double-ended toy, leaving a gap in Henrietta's back level with the stitching guideline made in Step 1 of Henrietta and wide enough to turn the toy and the skirt right side out. Carefully trim the seam allowance to ⅛ in./3 mm (felt doesn't fray, so the likelihood of the fabric tearing at the seams is minimal) and snip into the sharp corners of Reynard's ears.

5 Gently turn the toy right side out and press out any creases in the skirt panel. Carefully stuff the figures. Tuck in the exposed seam allowance and neatly slipstitch the opening closed, using the pre-stitched lines as a guide (see page 103).

3 With right sides together, aligning all straight, raw cdgcs, lay Henrietta on top of Reynard, sandwiching the skirt in between them. Pin, baste (tack), and machine stitch the central "waist" seam. Press open the waist seam, making sure that the felt and gingham seams are lying as flat as possible.

6 To finish, over-stitch the wing to Henrietta's body and join the open ends of the skirt with small, neat slipstitching.

4. Creature comforts

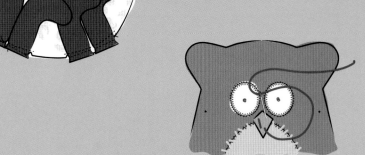

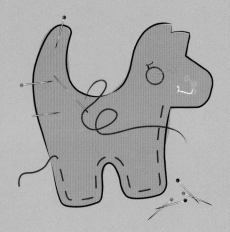

PRESTON THE PANDA

Undoubtedly, the cutest creature on the planet! The vibrant and optimistic Oriental floral print provides a dramatic contrast with the panda's black-and-white face. You can either make it as a soft toy or sew a ribbon on the back and turn it into a decoration that will look very pretty hanging in any child's bedroom.

YOU WILL NEED

- Patterns 01–05 and template 01 from the pull-out sheet
- 8 x 16 in. (20 x 40 cm) white velvet for head
- 12 x 12 in. (30 x 30 cm) black velvet for paws, eye patches, ears, and tail
- 12 x 16 in. (30 x 40 cm) floral print fabric for body
- 4 x 4 in. (10 x 10 cm) fusible bonding web

- 1 yd (100 cm) satin ribbon, ½ in. (10 mm) wide
- Pink and black stranded embroidery floss (cotton)
- Hollow fiber filling

Other stuff
- Sewing machine
- Needle and matching sewing threads
- Glue

- Take ⅜-in. (1-cm) seam allowances throughout unless otherwise stated.

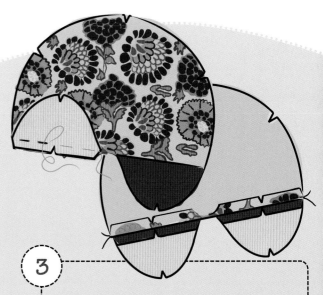

1 Using the patterns, cut out two heads from white velvet, and four paw pieces, four ears, and two tail pieces from black velvet. Cut two body pieces from floral print fabric. Transfer all markings from the paper patterns to the fabric. Remove the paper patterns.

2 With right sides together, pin, baste (tack), and machine stitch together the two ears and the tail. Trim the seam allowances to ¼ in. (5 mm) and cut little notches around all the curved edges. Turn the ears and tail right side out. Put the ears to one side. Stuff the tail and close the opening by working a few machine stitches close to the raw edge.

3

With right sides together, matching the balance marks, pin the front paws to the front body section. Baste (tack) and machine stitch together. Press open the seam. Repeat for the back section.

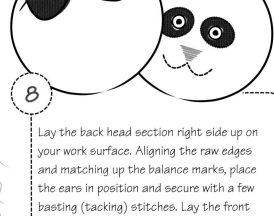

4 Lay the back body section right side up on your work surface. Fold the hanging ribbon in half lengthwise and place it in position, aligning the folded edge of the ribbon with the raw edge of the body. Secure with a few basting (tacking) stitches. Attach the stuffed tail in the same way, making sure you match up the balance marks.

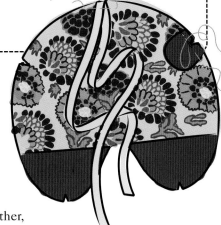

8 Lay the back head section right side up on your work surface. Aligning the raw edges and matching up the balance marks, place the ears in position and secure with a few basting (tacking) stitches. Lay the front head section on top, right side down. Pin, baste (tack), and machine stitch all around, leaving a gap at the side of the head to turn the toy right side out. Trim the seam allowance to ¼ in. (5 mm) and cut notches all around the edges.

5 With right sides together, aligning the raw edges, lay the front body section on top of the back section. Pin, baste (tack), and machine stitch all around, leaving a gap at the top right-hand side to turn the body right side out. Trim the seam allowance to ¼ in. (5 mm) and cut notches into the seam allowance around all the curved edges.

6 Turn the body right side out and stuff with hollow fiber filling. Tuck in the seam allowance around the opening and neatly slipstitch the opening closed (see page 103).

7 Lightly transfer the face markings onto the right side of one of the head sections. Following the manufacturer's instructions, iron the fusible bonding web to the wrong side of the black velvet for the eye patches. Draw around the eye-patch template twice on the paper side of the bonding web and cut out. Appliqué (see page 105) the eye patches to the head. Embroider the other features, using a French knot for the pupils of the eyes, satin stitch for the nose, and backstitch for the mouth (see page 104).

9 Turn the head right side out and stuff it with hollow fiber filling. Tuck in the seam allowance around the opening and neatly slipstitch the opening closed (see page 103).

10 Attach the head to the body, either by sewing small, neat stitches at the front and back, or by using a glue gun.

MYFANAWY THE SHEEP

Born in a small Welsh village surrounded by mountains and sweeping valleys, I remember sheep often getting into our garden to munch on the flowers—much to my mother's annoyance. But Myfanawy is not just any old sheep: she was inspired by childhood memories of trips to local farms with my sister and father to help out with lamb-feeding in springtime.

YOU WILL NEED

- Pattern pieces P1–P2 and templates P1–P4 from the pull-out sheet
- 12 x 20 in. (30 x 50 cm) imitation sheepskin for body and tail
- 6½ x 9 in. (16 x 22 cm) black brushed cotton for head
- Four 4¾ x 7-in. (12 x 18-cm) pieces of black brushed cotton for legs
- 3½ x 4¾ in. (8 x 12 cm) thick black wool felt for ears

- Pink and brown stranded embroidery floss (cotton) for features
- White and blue felt scraps for eyes
- Hollow fiber filling

Other stuff
- Sewing machine
- Needle and matching sewing threads
- Glue

- Take ⅜-in. (1-cm) seam allowances throughout unless otherwise stated.

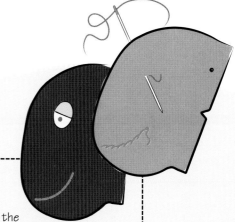

1 Pin the body pattern to the sheepskin fabric and cut out a left and a right body. Pin the head pattern to the black brushed cotton fabric and cut out a left and a right head. Remove the paper patterns.

2 Run a short row of machine stitches ⅜ in. (1 cm) in from the back of both back body pieces, as a guide for when finishing the toy after stuffing (see page 103).

3 Lightly transfer the face markings onto the right sides of the head pieces and embroider the mouth in pink backstitch (see page 104). Cut out small lozenge-shaped eyes from white felt and half-lozenge-shaped lids from blue felt, and glue them to the heads. Embroider the pupil of each eye in brown floss (cotton), using a French knot.

4 Place the ear template on felt, draw around it twice, and cut out. Fold the ears in half lengthwise and secure the folds with machine stitches. Lay the finished head sections right side up on your work surface. Place the folded ears in the dot position on top, align the raw edges, and attach with a few machine stitches.

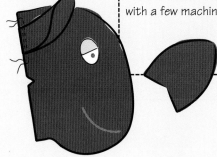

6 Lay one body piece right side up on your work surface. Place the legs in position and secure with a few machine stitches.

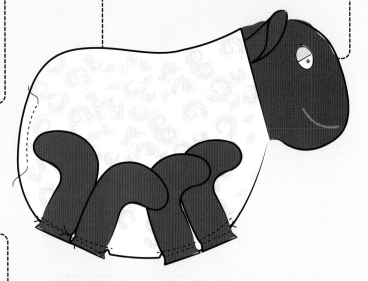

5 Fold one of the 4¾ x 7-in. (12 x 18-cm) rectangles of black cotton in half, aligning the short ends. Place the leg template on top and draw around it with tailor's chalk. Pin the layers together and carefully machine stitch along the line. Cut out, cutting ¼ in. (5 mm) beyond the stitching. Cut out little wedges along the curves, and turn right side out. Lightly stuff. Aligning the raw edges, close the opening with a line of machine stitches, ⅜ in. (1 cm) in from the raw edges. Repeat for the other legs.

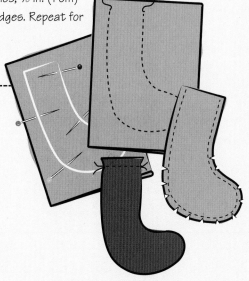

7 With right sides together, aligning the raw edges and making sure the legs and ears are neatly tucked inside, pin and baste (tack) the bodies together. Machine stitch all around, leaving a gap in the back wide enough to turn the toy right side out. Trim the seam allowance to ¼ in. (5 mm) and cut out little wedges around the curved edges. Turn the sheep right side out and stuff with hollow fiber filling. Tuck in the exposed seam allowance and neatly slipstitch the opening closed, using the pre-stitched lines as a guide (see page 103).

8 Place the tail template on top of two layers of sheepskin fabric right sides together and draw around it with tailor's chalk. Pin the layers in place and carefully machine stitch along the line. Trim the seam allowance to ¼ in. (5 mm), cut out little wedges along the curves, and turn right side out. Tuck in the exposed seam allowance by ⅜ in. (1 cm) and neatly slipstitch the opening closed. Hand stitch the tail to the sheep.

RUBY THE DACHSHUND

The luxurious coat of this precious pooch is made of jewel-toned velvet—hence her name, Ruby. An attractive dog collar and larger-than-life bone in felt adorn her elegant neck—you see, she never goes anywhere without a snack close at hand (or should I say, paw?). Her delectably cute nose is made from a fluffy pompom.

YOU WILL NEED

- Pattern pieces Q1–Q5 and templates Q1–Q2 from the pull-out sheet
- 20 x 36 in. (50 x 90 cm) cotton velvet for body, base, front legs (including ears), hind legs, and tail
- Pink and petrol-blue stranded embroidery floss (cotton) for features
- White felt scraps for eyes
- Fusible bonding web
- One small ready-made pompom for nose
- Double-thickness petrol-blue and lime-green felt for dog collar and bone
- Metallic gold string
- Hollow fiber filling

Other stuff

- Sewing machine
- Needle and matching sewing threads
- Glue
- Hole punch

- Take ⅜-in. (1-cm) seam allowances throughout unless otherwise stated.

1 Pin the paper pattern pieces to the cotton velvet fabric and cut out two body pieces, four feet, eight arms (four of these pieces will be used for the ears), two tails, and one base. Remove the paper patterns.

2

Run a short row of machine stitches ⅜ in. (1 cm) in from the back of both body pieces as a guide for when finishing the toy after stuffing (see page 103). Lightly transfer the face markings onto the right side of both body pieces and embroider the eyebrows and mouth in backstitch (see page 104), using pink floss (cotton) for the mouth and blue for the eyebrows. Back the felt for the eyes with fusible bonding web. Place the eye template on the felt, draw around it twice, and cut out. Appliqué (see page 105) the eyes in position, then embroider a large blue French knot in the center of each eye.

3

With right sides together and aligning the edges, pin, baste (tack), and machine stitch all around the tail, leaving the lower end open. Trim the seam allowance to ¼ in. (5 mm) and cut out little wedges around the curves Turn right side out and stuff with hollow fiber filling. Center the two seams and, aligning the raw edges, close the opening with machine stitches ¼ in. (5 mm) in from the edge. Put to one side.

4

With right sides together and aligning the edges, pin, baste (tack), and machine stitch all around both feet, leaving the slightly curved ends open. Trim the seam allowance to ¼ in. (5 mm) and cut out little wedges around the curves. Turn right side out and lightly stuff. Aligning the raw edges, close the openings with machine stitches ¼ in. (5 mm) in from the edge. Put to one side.

5 With right sides together and aligning the edges, place the eight arms together in pairs. Pin, baste (tack), and machine stitch all around, leaving a gap in the stitching wide enough to turn the piece right side out. Trim the seam allowance to ¼ in. (5 mm) and cut out little wedges around the curves. Turn all four pieces right side out. Lightly stuff two pieces; the other two will be used for the ears. Tuck in the seam allowance around the openings of all four pieces and neatly slipstitch the openings closed (see page 103). Put to one side.

6 With right sides together and aligning the raw edges, lay the back body section on top of the front section. Pin, baste (tack), and machine stitch all around, apart from the straight lower edges. Leave a gap in the stitching at the back seam of the body, wide enough to turn the toy right side out. Trim the seam allowance to ¼ in. (5 mm) and cut out little wedges around the curves.

7 Lay the base right side up on your work surface. Place the tail and the two stuffed hind legs in position and secure with machine stitches.

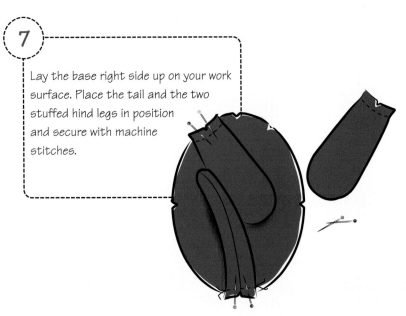

8 With right sides together, pin, baste (tack), and carefully machine stitch the base to the body of the dog, ensuring that all balance marks match and that the feet and tail are neatly tucked inside. Make small snips along the lower raw edges of the dog's body sections in order to make it easier to ease the straight edge around the curved edge of the base.

9 Trim all seam allowances to ¼ in. (5 mm) and cut notches around the curved edges. Turn the dog right side out and stuff with hollow fiber filling. Tuck in the seam allowance around the back-seam opening and neatly slipstitch the opening closed (see page 103), using the pre-stitched lines as a guide.

10 Using small, neat stitches, attach the arms and the ears (the two unstuffed arms) to the body. Glue on the pompom nose.

11 To make the dog collar, cut a 1 x 8-in. (2.5 x 20-cm) strip of double-thickness felt. Punch a hole halfway along the strip and ⅜ in. (1 cm) above one of the longer edges. Place the bone template on double-thickness felt, draw around it, and cut out. Punch a hole in the top. Attach the bone to the collar with metallic gold string. Wrap the collar around Ruby's neck and secure with a cross stitch at the back.

OSKAR THE OWL

Oskar is a very smart chap on both counts—brainpower and appearance. And he's a veritable ode to the autumnal woodland landscape in his natural, earthy hues. The subtle mix of textured fabrics (linen, felt, and tweed) is rustic yet refined, making this a toy that will appeal to all ages—and he's guaranteed to look just as good perched on a nursery shelf as he will nestling in between the cushions of an iconic Florence Knoll sofa.

YOU WILL NEED

- Pattern R1 and templates R1–R5 from the pull-out sheet
- 10½ x 16½ in. (26 x 42 cm) wool tweed for body
- 10½ x 16½ in. (26 x 42 cm) lightweight fusible interfacing
- 4¾ x 4¾ in. (12 x 12 cm) linen for breast
- Scrap of cream felt for eyes
- 4¾ x 6½ in. (12 x 16 cm) fusible bonding web

- 5½ x 5½ in. (14 x 14 cm) fawn double thickness felt for wings
- 3½ x 4¾ in. (8 x 12 cm) gold double thickness felt for feet and beak
- Brown and pale yellow stranded embroidery floss (cotton)
- 36 in. (90 cm) satin ribbon, ½ in. (10 mm) wide
- Hollow fiber filling

Other stuff
- Sewing machine
- Needle and matching sewing threads

- Take ⅜-in. (1-cm) seam allowances throughout unless otherwise stated.

1 Apply lightweight fusible interfacing to the wrong side of the tweed fabric to give it more body. Fold the body fabric in half, pin the pattern on top, and cut out, remembering to transfer all markings from the pattern to the fabric. Remove the paper pattern.

2 Run a short row of machine stitches ⅜ in. (1 cm) in from the bottom edge of both body pieces as a guide for when finishing the toy after stuffing (see page 103). Following the manufacturer's instructions, back the linen fabric for the breast and the cream felt for the eyes with fusible bonding web. Place the breast and eye templates on the relevant fabric, draw around them, and cut out. Place the foot and beak templates on the gold double-thickness felt, draw around them, cut out, and put to one side. Appliqué (see page 105) the breast and eyes to the body.

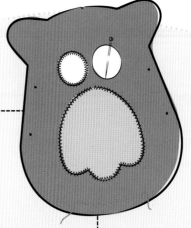

3 Work a small French knot (see page 104) in the center of each eye. Embellish the outline of the breast with haphazardly placed straight stitches in pale yellow embroidery floss (cotton). Place the beak in position and secure by working two straight stitches in brown embroidery floss (cotton) for the two nostrils.

5 With right sides together, aligning the raw edges and ensuring the wings and hanging ribbon are neatly tucked inside, lay the front body section on top of the back section. Pin, baste (tack), and machine stitch all around, leaving a gap in the base wide enough to turn the toy right side out. Trim the seam allowance to ¼ in. (5 mm) and cut out little wedges around the curved edges.

6 Turn the body right side out and stuff with hollow fiber filling. Tuck in the seam allowance around the opening and neatly slipstitch the opening closed (see page 103).

4 Place the wing template on the piece of fawn double-thickness felt, draw around it twice, cut out, and put to one side. Lay the back piece right side up on your work surface. Place the wings in position and secure with a few machine stitches. Fold the hanging ribbon in half lengthwise and place it in position, aligning the folded edge of the ribbon with the raw edge of the head. Secure with a few machine stitches.

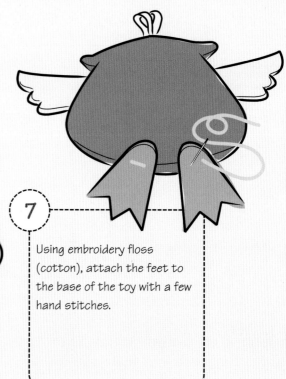

7 Using embroidery floss (cotton), attach the feet to the base of the toy with a few hand stitches.

CONCHITA THE CHICKEN

This chick is as spicy as a hot tamale! And she's dressed in her eclectic best with bright poster-paint colors, naïve florals, folksy trims, and embroideries. Look out for vintage oddments and embroideries that can be re-used for appliqués—note the ethnic-style feather stitchery on the heart-shaped wings, which was recycled from a retro apron.

YOU WILL NEED

- Patterns S1–S3 and templates S1–S3 from the pull-out sheet
- 13 x 24½ in. (32 x 62 cm) floral print cotton fabric for body
- 5½ x 6½ in. (14 x 16 cm) plain cotton fabric for base
- 5½ x 13 in. (14 x 32 cm) plain cotton fabric for head
- 2½ x 4¾ in. (6 x 12 cm) plain cotton fabric for beak appliqué
- 2½ x 4¾ in. (6 x 12 cm) fusible bonding web
- Four 9-in. (22-cm) lengths of jumbo rickrack

- Two 4¾ x 4¾ in. (12 x 12 cm) pieces of vintage embroidery
- 9½-in. (24-cm) square of fusible bonding web
- 7-in. (18-cm) length of scalloped eyelet trim, 2 in. (5 cm) wide
- 24-in. (60-cm) length of gingham ribbon ⅝ in. (15 mm) wide
- Scraps of felt for eyes

- Orange and turquoise stranded embroidery floss (cotton)
- Hollow fiber filling

Other stuff
- Sewing machine
- Needle and matching sewing threads

- Take ⅜-in. (1-cm) seam allowances throughout unless otherwise stated.

1 Pin the pattern pieces to the relevant fabrics. Cut out one front and one back body, two heads, and one base. Remove all the paper patterns.

2 Using a pencil, lightly transfer the rickrack positions onto the right side of the body pieces. Run a short row of machine stitches ⅜ in. (1 cm) in from the side of both body pieces as a guide for when finishing the toy after stuffing (see page 103). Back the vintage embroidery scrap with fusible bonding web. Place the heart template for the wing on the embroidery, draw around it twice, and cut out. Appliqué (see page 105) the wings to the body pieces. Place the lengths of rickrack in position across the lower edges of the body pieces and machine stitch in place.

3

Lay both head sections right side up on your work surface. Back the felt for the eyes and the cotton for the beak with fusible bonding web. Draw around the eye and beak templates, cut out, and fix in place with a hot iron. Work a single cross stitch (see page 104) in the center of each eye and star stitches set in a circle around each eye. Finish the wide end of each beak with small zigzag stitches.

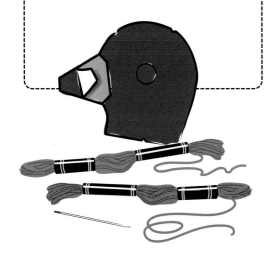

4

To make the comb, double hem the short ends of the eyelet trim, turning over ¼ in. (5 mm) and then another ¼ in. (5 mm). Pleat the strip to measure 2 in. (5 cm) and hold the pleats in place with machine stitches. Place the gathered comb on the head and machine stitch in position.

5

With right sides together, pin, baste (tack), and machine stitch the heads to the body pieces. Press open the seam allowances.

6 Lay one body section right side up on your work surface. Fold the neck ribbon in half lengthwise and place it in position, aligning the folded edge of the ribbon with the raw edge of the head. Secure with a few machine stitches.

7 With right sides together and aligning the raw edges, lay the back body section on top of the front section. Pin, baste (tack), and machine stitch all around, leaving a gap in the lower tail wide enough to turn the toy right side out.

8 With right sides together, pin, baste (tack), and carefully machine stitch the base to the body of the chicken, ensuring that all balance marks match and that the comb and ribbon are neatly tucked inside. Make small snips along the lower raw edges of the chicken body sections in order to make it easier to ease the body around the curved edge of the base.

9 Trim all seam allowances to ¼ in. (5 mm) and cut notches around the curved edges. Turn the chicken right side out and stuff with hollow fiber filling. Tuck in the seam allowance around the opening and neatly slipstitch the opening closed (see page 103), using the pre-stitched lines as a guide. To finish, tie the ribbon in a bow around Conchita's neck.

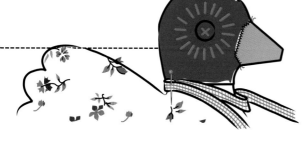

SPOT THE DOG

Spot's a frisky little fellow—and who could possibly resist his piercing blue eyes, cheeky pink nose, stumpy legs, and pointed tail? Although he's small in size, he's big in personality and possesses far more character than any store-bought toy. Made in the softest wool fabric, Spot is destined to become one of the most endearing and best-loved members of the nursery.

YOU WILL NEED

- Pattern T1 and template T1 from the pull-out sheet
- 10½ x 21½ in. (26 x 54 cm) lightweight wool fabric for body
- Scrap of fawn-colored felt for eye patch
- Fusible bonding web
- Pink, blue, and white stranded embroidery floss (cotton)
- Hollow fiber filling

Other stuff

- Sewing machine
- Needle and matching sewing threads

- Take ⅜-in. (1-cm) seam allowances throughout unless otherwise stated.

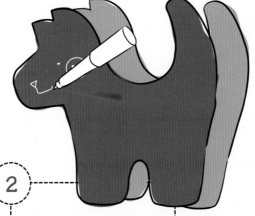

1 Fold the body fabric in half, pin the body pattern on top, and cut out. Remember to transfer all markings from the paper pattern to the fabric. Remove the paper pattern.

2 Lightly transfer the face markings onto the right side of one of the body pieces (see page 100).

3 Following the manufacturer's instructions, back the felt scrap for the eye patch with fusible bonding web. Draw around the shape for the eye patch on the paper side of the bonding web and cut out. Appliqué the eye patch to the right side of one body piece (see page 105). Embroider the facial features, using backstitch (mouth), satin stitch (nose), and French knots (eye and muzzle)—see page 104.

4

With right sides together, aligning the raw edges, pin, baste (tack), and machine stitch all the way around, leaving a gap below the tail wide enough to turn the toy right side out. Trim the seam allowance to ¼ in. (5 mm) and cut little notches into the seam allowance around all the curved edges.

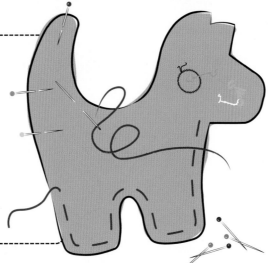

5 Turn the body right side out and stuff with hollow fiber filling. Tuck in the seam allowance around the opening and neatly slipstitch the opening closed (see page 103 Step 3).

5. Divine dollies

BRONWYN

Bronwyn is bright and zany and loves combining lots of different colors and patterns in her outfits. Floral fabrics are her absolute favorite, and she's also a big fan of blues and pinks—so this colorful combination, teamed with stripy leggings, was definitely meant to be.

YOU WILL NEED

- Pattern pieces U1–U2 and templates U1–U8 from the pull-out sheet
- 14 x 20 in. (35 x 50 cm) plain fabric for body and back legs
- 8 x 8 in. (20 x 20 cm) striped fabric for front legs
- 8 x 8 in. (20 x 20 cm) floral print fabric for appliqué dress and pockets
- 4¾ x 4¾ in. (12 x 12 cm) spotted fabric for appliqué bib and collar
- 4 x 8 in. (10 x 20 cm) plain fabric for appliqué shoes

- 6 x 8 in. (15 x 20 cm) brown felt for appliqué hair
- Scraps of white, pink, and turquoise felt for eyes and mouth
- Scraps of purple felt for buttons
- 12-in. (30-cm) square of fusible bonding web

- Hollow fiber filling

Other stuff
- Sewing machine
- Needle and matching sewing threads

- Take ⅜-in. (1-cm) seam allowances throughout unless otherwise stated.

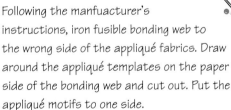

1 Following the manfuacturer's instructions, iron fusible bonding web to the wrong side of the appliqué fabrics. Draw around the appliqué templates on the paper side of the bonding web and cut out. Put the appliqué motifs to one side.

2 Pin the body and leg patterns to the plain fabric and cut out, remembering to transfer all markings from the pattern to the fabric. Cut two bodies and two legs (left and right). Remove the paper patterns. Pin the leg pattern to the striped fabric and cut out two legs (left and right). Remove the paper patterns.

3 Lay one body section right side up on your work surface and, using a hot iron, carefully fuse the appliqué motifs in place one by one (see page 105). Start with the dress, then the bib, then the collar, and finish with the patch pockets. Satin stitch or close zigzag stitch the raw edges of each appliqué motif.

4 Apply the hair, eyes, and mouth in the same way. Using small backstitches (see page 104), stitch a nose and a hairgrip.

5 Apply the shoe appliqués to the striped fabric legs, again satin stitching or zig-zag stitching the raw edges.

6 With right sides together, pin, baste (tack), and machine stitch the front and back of the legs together. Trim the seam allowance to ¼ in. (5 mm) and cut notches around the curved edges. Turn the legs right side out and stuff with hollow fiber filling.

7 Lay the front body section right side up on your work surface. Place the stuffed legs in position on top, aligning the raw edges and making sure that the balance marks match up. Secure with a few basting (tacking) stitches. With right sides together, aligning the raw edges, lay the back body section on top of the front section. Pin, baste (tack), and machine stitch all around, leaving a gap at the side to turn the doll right side out. Trim the seam allowance to ¼ in. (5 mm) and cut notches around the edges.

8 Turn the doll right side out. Stuff with hollow fiber filling. Tuck in the seam allowance around the opening and neatly slipstitch the opening closed (see page 103).

9 Cut two ⅝-in. (1.5-cm) circles and two ⅜-in. (1-cm) circles of felt. Hand stitch the larger buttons onto the bib and the smaller ones onto the shoe straps. Cut out a little felt flower and stitch it to the hairgrip.

ROSIE

As pretty as a summer garden, flowers abound on this sweet little rag doll. Delicate embroidered lawn and muslin mix with pin dots and floral sprigs. Silk petals at the waist and head echo the fine hand embroidered florals on the little apron, which is fashioned from a vintage handkerchief. Bloomin' gorgeous!

YOU WILL NEED

- Pattern pieces V1–V5 and template V1 from the pull-out sheet
- 10½ x 12 in. (26 x 30 cm) spotted fabric for body and arms
- 4¾ x 4¾ in. (12 x 12 cm) flesh-colored fabric for face and hands
- 4¾ x 4¾ in. (12 x 12 cm) contrast plain fabric for back of head
- 12 x 12 in. (30 x 30 cm) floral print fabric for legs
- Pink, red, and black felt for facial features
- Hollow fiber filling
- 8 x 13 in. (20 x 32 cm) muslin for skirt
- Embroidered handkerchief for apron
- 28 in. (70 cm) satin ribbon, ¼ in. (5 mm) wide
- 3 x 40 in. (100 cm) lengths of pure wool light worsted (double knitting) yarn for hair
- 2 small silk flowers

Other stuff

- Sewing machine
- Needle and matching sewing threads
- Hole punch
- Glue

- Take ⅜-in. (1-cm) seam allowances throughout unless otherwise stated.

1 Pin the head, body, hand, arm, and leg patterns to the relevant fabrics. Cut out two heads, two body pieces, four hands and arms, and four legs. Remove the paper patterns.

2 Lightly transfer the face markings onto the right side of the flesh-colored face piece. Cut out small circles of felt for the eyes, mouth, and rosy cheeks (a hole punch is ideal for this) and glue them to the head. To make a looped fringe, take three 2½-in. (6-cm) strands of wool, fold them in half, lay them side by side at the top center of the head, and baste (tack) in place.

3 With right sides together, pin, baste (tack), and machine stitch together the two sets of head and body pieces. Press open the seams.

4 With right sides together, aligning the raw edges, lay the back body on top of the front body. Pin, baste (tack), and machine stitch all around, leaving the lower edge open. Trim the seam allowance to ¼ in. (5 mm) and cut notches along the curved edge.

5 With right sides together, pin, baste (tack), and machine stitch each hand to an arm. Trim the seam allowance to ¼ in. (5 mm) and press open the seam. With right sides together, aligning the raw edges, lay one back arm on top of a front arm. Pin, baste (tack), and machine stitch all around, leaving the straight-edged end open. Trim the seam allowance to ¼ in. (5 mm) and cut notches along the curved edge. Repeat for the other arm and the legs.

6 Turn both arms and legs right side out and stuff with hollow fiber filling. Tuck in the seam allowance around the openings and neatly slipstitch the openings closed (see page 103).

7

Stuff the body cavity with hollow fiber filling. Tuck in the seam allowance around the opening. Lay the doll right side up on your work surface, insert the legs, and pin them in position, aligning all raw edges inside. Pin, baste (tack), and machine stitch the opening closed, making sure both legs are neatly sandwiched between the front and back body panels.

8

Using small, neat hand stitches, attach an arm to each side of the body, ⅜ in. (1 cm) below the seam between the head and body.

9 To make the ponytail braid, take three 40-in. (100-cm) strands of yarn, fold each one in half, and braid (plait) them together. Knot each end securely and tie with a small ribbon bow. Using glue or small hand stitches, attach the braid to the head, covering the seam line between the front and back head pieces. Attach a fabric flower at the hairline.

10 To make the skirt, cut an 8 x 13-in. (20 x 32-cm) rectangle of muslin. Fold the fabric in half, aligning the short ends. Machine stitch across the short end and press the seam open. Fold the top and bottom edges over by ⅜ in. (1 cm), press, and finish with picot edges (see page 106). Fold the skirt over lengthwise, with the picot edge of the upper layer ⅜ in. (1 cm) higher than that of the under layer. Press the fold and, using a running stitch (see page 104), gather the skirt. Slip the skirt onto the doll and secure with hand stitches.

11 To make the apron, cut off the corner of an embroidered handkerchief. Fold the cut edge over by ⅜ in. (1 cm) and picot the edge (see page 106). Gather up, lay the apron over the skirt, and stitch in place. Wrap a ribbon twice around the waist and tie in a bow at back. Decorate the waist with a fabric flower. Attach a ribbon bow to the body.

ELOISE

Long and lanky but ever so lovely, Eloise is the ultimate waif. Her flaxen hair is made from twisted silk and mohair yarn, while her gorgeous confetti-spot slip dress is crêpe de chine trimmed with vintage crocheted lace. This doll is simple yet stunning, proving without doubt that "less is more." The detachable dress is just a tube with a drawstring casing, so numerous different styles can be made with ease.

YOU WILL NEED

- Pattern pieces W1–W3 and template W1 from the pull-out sheet
- 14 x 28-in. (35 x 70-cm) flesh-colored fabric for body, arms, and legs
- 10½ x 13-in. (26 x 32-cm) silk spotted fabric for dress
- 13 in. (32 cm) crocheted lace, 2½ in. (6 cm) wide
- Lilac felt for mouth
- Pink stranded embroidery floss (cotton) for mouth
- Brown and white stranded embroidery floss (cotton) for eyes and beauty spot
- 8¾ yd (8 m) silk/mohair twisted yarn for hair
- Hollow fiber filling
- Wired ribbon for hair
- 2 two-hole buttons, ⅜ in. (1 cm) in diameter
- 32 in. (80 cm) silk ribbon, ¼ in. (5 mm) wide

Other stuff

- Sewing machine
- Needle and matching sewing threads

- Take ⅜-in. (1-cm) seam allowances throughout unless otherwise stated.

1 Pin the body, arm, and leg patterns to the flesh-colored fabric. Cut out two body pieces, four arms, and four legs. Remove the paper patterns.

2

Lightly transfer the face markings to the right side of one body piece (see page 100). Cut out a small heart-shaped mouth from lilac felt and stitch it in place. Embroider the facial features, using straight stitch for the eyebrows, tiny satin stitches for the eyes, and a single stitch for the white of the eyes and a beauty spot on one cheek (see page 104).

3

Place the other body piece right side up and machine stitch a 3¾-in. (9-cm) vertical line down the center of the head from the top, as a guideline for laying the strands of yarn for the hair. Cut ten 8-in. (20-cm) strands and lay them horizontally one by one over the guideline. Carefully machine stitch in place.

4

Once the back of the head is covered with strands of yarn, stretch the yarn taut and carefully machine stitch around the head, ¼ in. (5 mm) in from the raw edge, to secure the yarn in place. Trim off any excess yarn.

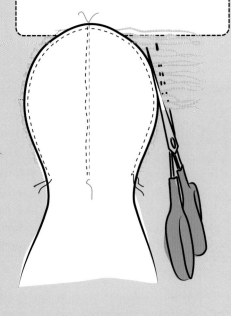

5 With right sides together, aligning the raw edges, lay the back body on top of the front body. Pin, baste (tack), and machine stitch all around, leaving the lower edge open. Trim the seam allowance to ¼ in. (5 mm) and cut notches along the curved edge.

6 With right sides together, aligning the raw edges, lay one back arm on top of a front arm. Pin, baste (tack), and machine stitch all around, leaving the straight end open. Trim the seam allowance to ¼ in. (5 mm) and cut notches along the curved edge. Repeat for the other arm and the legs.

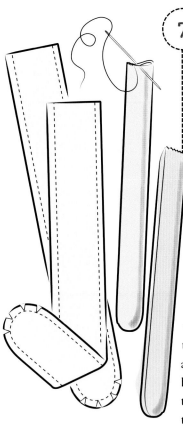

7

Turn both arms and legs right side out and stuff with hollow fiber filling. Tuck in the seam allowance around the openings and neatly slipstitch the openings closed (see page 103).

8 Stuff the body cavity with hollow fiber filling. Tuck in the seam allowance around the opening. Lay the doll right side up on your work surface, insert the legs, and pin them in position, aligning all raw edges inside. Pin, baste (tack), and machine stitch the opening closed, making sure that both legs are neatly sandwiched between the front and back body panels.

9

Stitch the arms firmly to the body, using small, two-hole buttons and embroidery floss (cotton). This will allow the limbs to be moved into different positions.

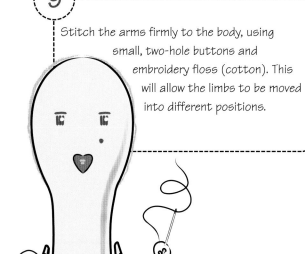

10

To make the loose hair, take nine 24-in. (60-cm) strands of yarn and lay them side by side. Carefully machine stitch through the yarns at the halfway point. Lay this band of yarns over the back of the head and hand stitch it securely in place, using the center stitches from Step 3 as a guide. Tie a length of wired ribbon in a bow around four or five strands on one side of the head to finish.

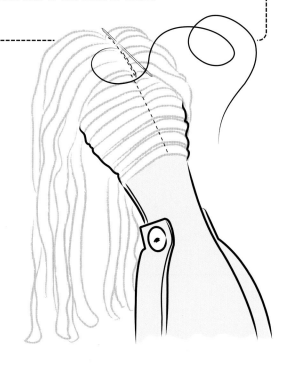

11 To make the dress, cut a 10½ x 13-in. (26 x 32-cm) rectangle of spotted silk fabric. Place the silk right side up, with the crocheted lace along one long edge, aligning the edges. Machine stitch the lace to the silk, using small zigzag stitches. Carefully trim away the silk underneath the lace.

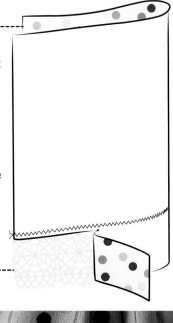

12 Fold the silk in half, right sides together, aligning the short ends. Machine stitch and press the seam open. Along the top edge, fold over ⅝ in. (1.5 cm) to the wrong side and press. Machine stitch along the edge, ⅜ in. (1 cm) from the fold, stitching through both layers to form a drawstring casing.

13 Thread a large-eyed darning needle with the silk ribbon, push it through the outer layer of fabric at the center front, pass it through the casing, and pull it out again, leaving a small gap between the entry and exit points. Slip the tube dress onto the doll, pull the drawstring tight, and make a bow. Secure the top of the dress to the doll's back with a few hand stitches.

ANTONELLA

Her hair brushed back and neatly tied in a ponytail, attired in a daintily be-ribboned and lace-edged bed jacket and bloomers, this young lady is elegance personified. Amplifying the ladylike charm of her outfit are chic black bed stockings trimmed with satin bows.

YOU WILL NEED

- Pattern pieces X1–X7 and template X1 from the pull-out sheet
- 16 x 33½ in. (40 x 85 cm) white cotton fabric for body, arms, and upper legs
- 10 x 17¾ in. (25 x 45 cm) black cotton fabric for lower legs and scalp appliqué
- Red and black felt scraps for features
- Hollow fiber filling
- Black stranded embroidery floss (cotton) for ponytail
- 21¾ x 28 in. (55 x 70 cm) ivory linen for bed jacket and bloomers

- 28 in. (70 cm) satin ribbon, ⅝ in. (15 mm) wide
- 52 in. (130 cm) crocheted lace trim, ⅜ in. (10 mm) wide
- 48 in. (120 cm) jacquard ribbon, ¼ in. (5 mm) wide for waist tie and hair bow
- Two ready-made satin bows for feet
- 28 in. (70 cm) floral jacquard ribbon, ¾ in. (20 mm) wide

Other stuff
- Sewing machine
- Needle and matching sewing threads
- Hole punch
- Glue

- Take ⅜-in. (1-cm) seam allowances throughout unless otherwise stated.

1 Pin the doll pattern pieces to the relevant fabrics. Cut out two body pieces, four arms, and four upper legs from white cotton fabric, and four lower legs and two scalps from black cotton fabric. Transfer all markings from the paper patterns to the fabric. Remove the paper patterns.

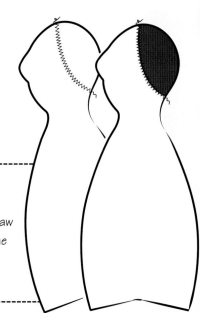

2 Using small, close zigzag machine stitches and sewing close to the raw edge, stitch the scalp pieces to the right side of the body sections.

3 With right sides facing, aligning the raw edges, put the left- and right-hand sides of the body together. Pin, baste (tack), and machine stitch all around, leaving the lower edges open. Trim the seam allowance to ¼ in. (5 mm) and cut out little wedges along the curved edge. Turn the body right side out and press.

4 Cut out small circles of felt for the eyes and mouth—a hole punch is ideal for this job—and fix them to the head with glue.

5 With right sides together, aligning the raw edges, lay a back arm on top of a front arm. Pin, baste (tack), and machine stitch all around, leaving the straight-edged end open. Trim the seam allowance to ¼ in. (5 mm) and cut out little wedges along the curved edge. Turn the arm right side out and stuff. Repeat for the other arm. Put to one side.

6 With right sides together, pin, baste (tack), and machine stitch the upper legs to the lower legs. Press open the seam allowances.

7 With right sides together, aligning the raw edges, lay the inside leg on the outside leg. Pin, baste (tack), and machine stitch all around, leaving the straight-edged end open. Repeat for the other leg. Trim the seam allowance to ¼ in. (5 mm), cut out little wedges around the curved edges, and turn both legs right side out.

8 Stuff the legs up to the "knee" seam and sink a row of machine stitches through the seams, before stuffing the upper part of the legs.

9 Stuff the body cavity, turning the lower raw edges under by ⅜ in. (1 cm). Lay the doll right side up on your work surface, insert the legs, and pin them in position, aligning all raw edges inside. Pin, baste (tack), and machine stitch the opening closed, making sure that both legs are neatly sandwiched between the front and back body panels.

10 Tuck the top, raw edges of the arms in by ⅜ in. (1 cm) and hand stitch them to the body with small, neat stitches.

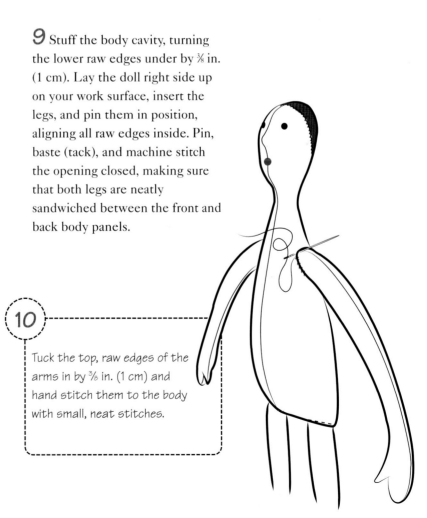

11 To make the ponytail, take twenty 6-in. (15-cm) strands of embroidery floss (cotton) and lay them side by side. Tie them together securely at the halfway point. Hand stitch them to the base of the scalp at the back of the head. Tie in a bow, with a 10-in. (25-cm) length of ¼-in. (5 mm) jacquard ribbon.

12 Cut two bloomer legs from linen fabric. Lay them right side up on your work surface and machine stitch a jacquard and a satin ribbon in place on each one. Pin a length of crocheted lace along each hem, aligning the edges, and machine stitch the lace to the linen using small zigzag stitches. Carefully trim away the linen underneath the lace.

13 With right sides together, machine stitch the two parts of the bloomers together along the front and back crotch.

14 Fold the bloomers so that the crotch seams are lying on top of each other and machine stitch the inner legs.

15 Fold the top edge of the bloomers over to the wrong side by ⅜ in. (1 cm) and press. Machine stitch through both layers to form a drawstring casing. Thread a needle with embroidery floss (cotton), push it through the upper layer of fabric at the center front, pass it through the casing, and pull it out again, leaving a small gap between the entry and exit points. Cut the doubled thread, leaving a long piece on each side and securing each end with a knot.

16 Cut two front and one back bed jacket piece from linen. With right sides together, machine stitch the front pieces to the back piece along the upper sleeves. Press open the seams.

18 With right sides together, fold the two front panels on top of the back panel and machine stitch together along both side and underarm edges. Press open the seams and turn the jacket right side out.

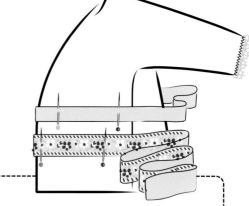

19 Pin lengths of jacquard and satin ribbon in position along the front and back panels of the bed jacket. Machine stitch in place. Pin a length of crocheted lace along the jacket hem, aligning the edges. Machine stitch the lace to the linen, using small zigzag stitches. Carefully trim away the linen underneath the lace.

20 Pin a length of crocheted lace along the neck and front openings of the bed jacket, aligning the edges. Machine stitch the lace to the linen, using small zigzag stitches. Carefully trim away the linen underneath the lace.

21 To finish, dress the doll and tie a 30-in. (80-cm) length of jacquard ribbon around the waist to keep the jacket in place.

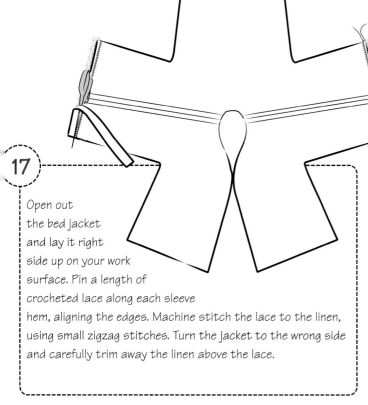

17 Open out the bed jacket and lay it right side up on your work surface. Pin a length of crocheted lace along each sleeve hem, aligning the edges. Machine stitch the lace to the linen, using small zigzag stitches. Turn the jacket to the wrong side and carefully trim away the linen above the lace.

TIPPI & TILLY,
THE TOPSY-TURVY GIRLS

The "dual-identity" doll dates back to before the American Civil War and is believed to have originated on Southern plantations. The dolls can be dressed as characters from fairy tales, such as Cinderella (before and after she meets Prince Charming), or opposites such as rich and poor, or simply with contrasting expressions—happy and sad.

YOU WILL NEED

For red-haired doll
- Pattern pieces Y1–Y3 from the pull-out sheet
- 8 x 12 in. (20 x 30 cm) calico for head and arms
- 12 x 16 in. (30 x 40 cm) colored cotton fabric for body
- 50 in. (125 cm) narrow vintage lace trim
- 30 in. (75 cm) wide vintage lace trim
- ¼-in. (5 mm) ribbon for bodice front bow and hair trim
- 13 x 24½ in. (32 x 62 cm) striped fabric for skirt
- One 2-oz (50g) ball pure wool light worsted (double knitting) yarn, approx. length 135 yd (125 m), for hair

For brunette doll
- Patterns Y1–Y3 from the pull-out sheet
- 8 x 12 in. (20 x 30 cm) calico (dyed in tea) for head and arms
- 12 x 16 in. (30 x 40 cm) colored cotton fabric for body
- 60 in. (150 cm) narrow vintage lace trim
- 24½ in. (62 cm) wide vintage lace trim
- ¼-in. (5 mm) ribbon for bodice front bow and hair trim
- 13 x 24½ in. (32 x 62 cm) striped fabric for skirt
- One 2-oz (50g) ball pure wool light worsted (double knitting) yarn, approx. length 135 yd (125 m), for hair

- 10 in. (25 cm) woven tape, 1 in. (25mm) wide, for skirt waistband
- 24½ in. (62 cm) wide vintage lace for skirt hem
- Stranded embroidery floss (cotton)
- Pink felt for mouths
- Hollow fiber filling

Other stuff
- Sewing machine
- Needle and matching sewing threads

- Take ⅜-in. (1-cm) seam allowances throughout unless otherwise stated.

1 To make the Red-haired doll, pin the head and arm patterns to the calico "skin" fabric. Cut out two heads and four arms. Pin the body pattern to the colored cotton fabric and cut out twice. Transfer all markings from the paper patterns to the fabric. Remove the paper patterns.

2 Lightly transfer the face markings to the right side of one of the head sections. Cut out a small heart-shaped mouth from pink felt and stitch or glue it to the head. Embroider the eyes and nose, using a French knot for the eyes and a single straight stitch for the nose (see page 104).

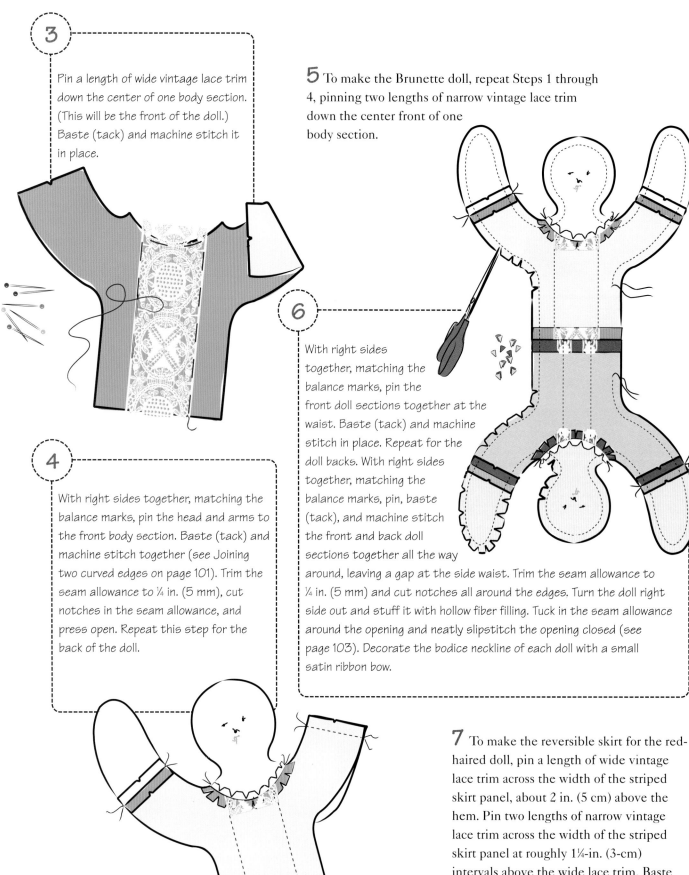

3 Pin a length of wide vintage lace trim down the center of one body section. (This will be the front of the doll.) Baste (tack) and machine stitch it in place.

4 With right sides together, matching the balance marks, pin the head and arms to the front body section. Baste (tack) and machine stitch together (see Joining two curved edges on page 101). Trim the seam allowance to ¼ in. (5 mm), cut notches in the seam allowance, and press open. Repeat this step for the back of the doll.

5 To make the Brunette doll, repeat Steps 1 through 4, pinning two lengths of narrow vintage lace trim down the center front of one body section.

6 With right sides together, matching the balance marks, pin the front doll sections together at the waist. Baste (tack) and machine stitch in place. Repeat for the doll backs. With right sides together, matching the balance marks, pin, baste (tack), and machine stitch the front and back doll sections together all the way around, leaving a gap at the side waist. Trim the seam allowance to ¼ in. (5 mm) and cut notches all around the edges. Turn the doll right side out and stuff it with hollow fiber filling. Tuck in the seam allowance around the opening and neatly slipstitch the opening closed (see page 103). Decorate the bodice neckline of each doll with a small satin ribbon bow.

7 To make the reversible skirt for the red-haired doll, pin a length of wide vintage lace trim across the width of the striped skirt panel, about 2 in. (5 cm) above the hem. Pin two lengths of narrow vintage lace trim across the width of the striped skirt panel at roughly 1¼-in. (3-cm) intervals above the wide lace trim. Baste (tack) and machine stitch in place.

8 To make the skirt for the brunette doll, pin a length of wide vintage lace trim across the width of the striped skirt panel, about 5 in. (13 cm) above the hem. Pin two lengths of narrow vintage lace trim across the width of the stripe skirt panel, one ⅝ in. (1.5 cm) above the wide lace and one ⅝ in. (1.5 cm) below. Baste (tack) and machine stitch in place.

10

Assemble the other skirt in the same way. Slip it over the first skirt, right sides together, aligning the hems and side seams. Pin and machine stitch together along the bottom edge and press open the seam. Turn the reversible skirt right side out, and then press the layers back onto each other. Topstitch along the hem edge, close to the seam between the skirt and the lace edging.

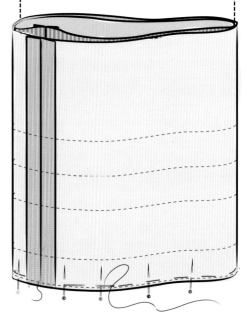

11 Making sure that both panels of the skirt are lying flat and the side seams match, align the raw edges of the waist and secure with machine stitches. Gather the skirt by hand or machine to approx. 7 in. (18 cm) (see page 102). Bind the raw edge of the skirt with the woven tape (see page 106) and put on doll. Pass the doll halfway through the skirt and attach the top edge of the skirt's binding to the doll's central "waist" seam with slipstitches.

12 Make the hair for each doll (see pages 108–109). Decorate the braids with ribbon bows.

9

Fold one skirt panel in half, right sides together. Pin, baste (tack), and machine stitch along the short side. Press open the seam. Turn right side out. Pin, then machine stitch a length of wide vintage lace edging along the raw edge of the hem.

How to make the perfect soft toy

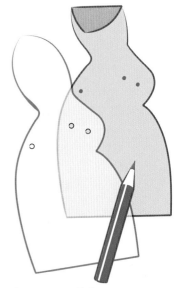

PATTERNS AND TEMPLATES

Transferring patterns

The patterns and templates you need to make the projects in this book are on pull-out sheets at the back. They are all full size, so you do not need to enlarge them. Trace the patterns you need, including all markings, onto tissue paper and cut them out, cutting along the solid line; a ⅜-in. (1-cm) seam allowance (stitching line) is included and is shown by a dotted line. Trace any templates that you need, including all markings, onto thin card.

Cutting out

Lay your fabric on a flat surface and smooth it out. To cut one fabric piece, place the paper pattern on single-thickness fabric, right side up.

To cut "mirror-image" left and right fabric pieces, place the paper pattern on double-thickness fabric, folding the fabric with right sides together.

To cut one symmetrical fabric piece from a half paper pattern, place the straight outer line of the paper pattern on the fold of the double-thickness fabric, folding the fabric with right sides together (as shown in the illustration on the left). Pin the paper pattern pieces to the fabric and cut along the edge, using sharp fabric scissors.

For templates, simply place them on the fabric and draw around them, using tailor's chalk or a "disappearing" fabric marker pen.

Pattern/template markings

DOTS

Dots indicate the attatchment points for limbs, hanging ribbon, pockets, and so on. Very fine dotted lines indicate areas that require embellishment with embroidery stitches. Fine lines mark the position of appliqués. After cutting, transfer all markings to the wrong side of the fabric before removing the paper pattern. Use pins, tailor's chalk or a "disappearing" fabric marker pen, as shown above.

BALANCE MARKS

Short, straight lines at the edges of the pattern indicate points that need to be matched across different pattern pieces. Transfer them from the paper pattern to the fabric, using tailor's chalk or snip into the fabric edges, making balance mark "notches" as shown below. It's also a good idea to snip the end of fold lines and center lines.

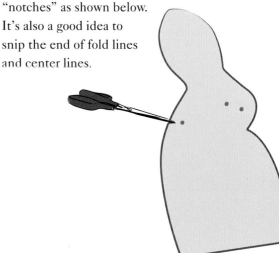

PROFESSIONAL SEWING TECHNIQUES

Joining a straight edge to a curved edge

Stay stitch the fabric piece $\frac{5}{16}$ in. (7 mm) in from the straight raw edge and cut small slits just short of the machine stitches. With right sides together and matching the balance marks, pin the snipped, pre-stitched edge to the curved edge, carefully working it around the curve, aligning the raw edges of both fabric pieces as you go. Baste (tack) and machine stitch together.

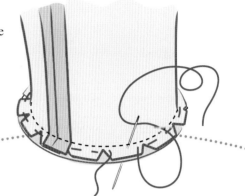

Joining two curved edges

A piece of fabric featuring a flat, curved seam is created by joining one fabric piece with an inward-curved edge to another fabric piece with an outward-curved edge.

1 Stay stitch the inward curve $\frac{5}{16}$ in. (7 mm) from the cut edge, cut small slits, and gently pull to straighten out the curve.

2 With right sides together, pin the pre-stitched inward curve to the outward curve, carefully working it around the outward curve, aligning the raw edges of both fabric pieces as you go. Baste (tack) and machine stitch together.

3 Cut wedge-shaped notches into both allowances and press open the seam.

Trimming seam allowances

To get the best possible shape to your toy, carefully trim down the seam allowance to about ¼ in. (5 mm) after stitching.

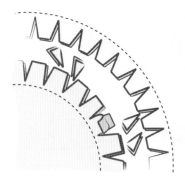

SNIPPING CURVED EDGES

On curved seams, cut wedge-shaped notches into the seam allowance after stitching, to maintain smooth curves when the toy is pulled right side out.

USING PINKING SHEARS

Using the saw-toothed blades of pinking shears to trim down seam allowances after stitching not only provides the required notches for curves but also minimizes any fraying of the seam allowances, which can sometimes occur when stuffing.

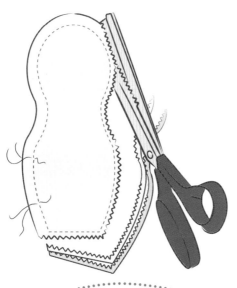

Pressing seams

Press seams open from the wrong side, unless instructed otherwise. (If you press seams from the right side, you may mark the fabric.) If you are stitching together two pieces that already have seams, press open the first seams, snip off the corners of the seam allowances, and align the seams exactly (if appropriate) when pinning the fabric pieces together.

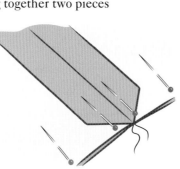

Gathering by machine

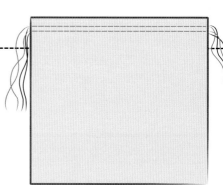

1 Using the longest straight stitch length, machine stitch two parallel lines ⅜ in. (1 cm) apart along the edge to be gathered.

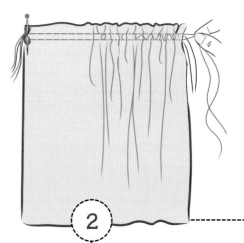

2 Secure all the threads at one end of the fabric with a pin and gently pull the two top threads at the other end to gather the fabric to the required length, making sure the gathers are even. Insert another pin to secure these threads.

3 When attaching the gathered fabric to another fabric piece, use a normal stitch length and machine stitch between the parallel lines of stitching to secure. Remove the parallel lines of stitching to finish.

Pre-stitched line guide for neat closures

This is a guide for finishing the toy after stuffing and an ideal method for closing an opening that is on a curve.

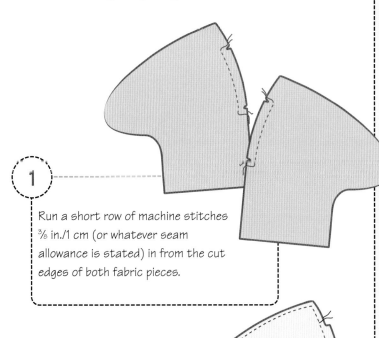

1 Run a short row of machine stitches ⅜ in./1 cm (or whatever seam allowance is stated) in from the cut edges of both fabric pieces.

2 Place the pieces to be joined right sides together. Start stitching at one end of the pre-stitched line, stitch all the way around the toy and stop at the other end of the pre-stitched line, leaving a gap in the stitching wide enough to turn the toy right side out. Do not trim the seam allowance around the pre-stitched guideline.

3 When slipstitching the opening closed, pass the needle under the pre-stitched lines, and pull together stitch by stitch, so they meet edge to edge; the finished, closed seam will be neat, flat, and without puckers.

TOP TIPS

Fabrics

Fabrics with a dense weave are a better choice for stuffed toys than thinner materials, because they hold their shape and there is less chance of seams splitting or fraying. Soft, compact quality wool felts are ideal, as are jersey knits and fleece. Textured tweed fabrics look great for "rustic" creatures, but you may need to iron a soft, lightweight interfacing to the reverse side of the fabric before cutting out the pattern pieces because this type of weave often has a loose and open structure. Rag dolls always look their best when made from 100 percent cotton calico, soft gabardine, or "quilters only." To create interesting "skin" tones, experiment by dyeing your base cloth in infusions of tea of various types, blends, and strengths.

Stuffing tools

A chopstick and the small, rounded end of a teaspoon are useful tools for reversing and stuffing a toy. A pair of good-quality, surgical tweezers (about 6 in./15 cm long) are ideal for pushing small lumps of stuffing into areas that are hard to get at, such as thumbs, noses, and the tips of tails.

Stuffing method

It's often a great temptation to stuff the toy in haste to see how it looks…don't! Push stuffing into the toy gently and loosely, bit by bit, to avoid lumps forming. Push and press the stuffing carefully into place and continue to add more until you have a firm and well-shaped figure.

Faces and features

Many craft books tell you to embroider the face and features of a toy after it has been stuffed and finished. Annoyingly, they do not explain how to conceal the knotted ends of the embroidery yarn. The only way to ensure this problem does not arise is to embroider the face beforehand. Most of the toys featured in this book have their features applied before they are sewn together, which is why the position of eyes, noses, and whiskers are clearly marked on the relevant patterns and templates, and require transferring.

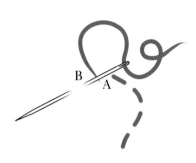

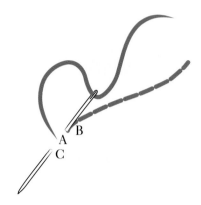

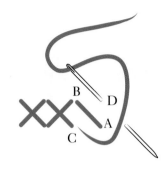

Running stitch

Work from right to left. Bring the needle up at A and back down through the fabric at B, then repeat several times, keeping the stitches and the spaces between them the same size.

Backstitch

Work from right to left. Bring the needle up at A, down at B, and up again at C. The distance between A and B should be the same as the distance between A and C. To begin the next stitch, insert the needle at A again.

Cross stitch

Bring the needle up at A and down at B, then up at C and down at D.

French knot

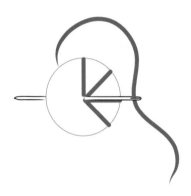

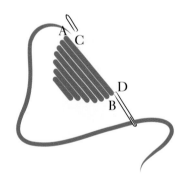

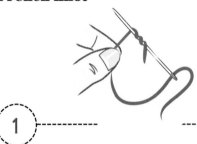

Star stitch

Work a series of straight stitches from the outside of a circle to the center point, to create a star shape.

Satin stitch

Work from left to right. Bring the needle up at A, down at B, up at C, and down at D. Place the stitches next to each other so that no fabric can be seen between them.

1 Bring the needle up from the back of the fabric to the front. Wrap the thread two or three times around the tip of the needle.

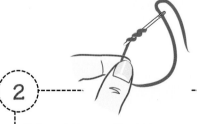

2 Reinsert the needle at the point where it first emerged, holding the wrapped threads with the thumbnail of your non-stitching hand.

104

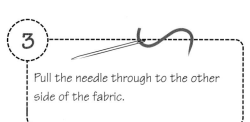

3 Pull the needle through to the other side of the fabric.

DECORATIVE EFFECTS

Appliqué

1 Trace the appliqué motif onto thin card and cut out.

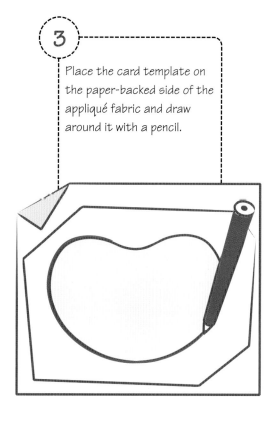

3 Place the card template on the paper-backed side of the appliqué fabric and draw around it with a pencil.

2 Cut a square of paper-backed fusible bonding web large enough to accommodate the appliqué motif. Lay the square on the wrong side of your appliqué fabric, adhesive side down, and press with a hot iron to heat bond.

4 Carefully cut out the motif and peel away the paper backing.

5 Place the motif, adhesive side down, on the main fabric and press with a hot iron to attach.

6 For a professional finish, machine stitch all around the motif with a small, dense zigzag stitch.

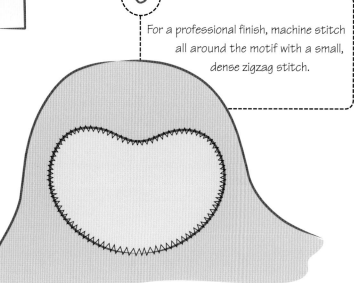

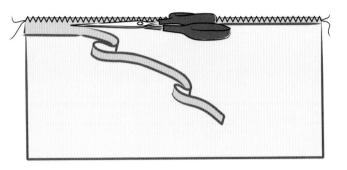

Bias binding

1 Fold a length of ready-made bias binding over lengthwise, gently steam-pressing as you fold.

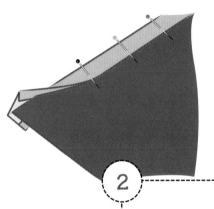

2 Neatly insert the raw edge of the fabric to be bound into the folded binding. Pin, baste (tack), and machine stitch in place. Note: "Shrink" the binding around corners with a steam iron before sewing to avoid puckering.

3 To make your own binding, cut a length of fabric 2 in. (5 cm) wide on the bias—that is, at an angle of 45° to the selvage (selvedge). Fold both long edges over to the wrong side so they meet in the exact center of the strip. Steam press the folds. Aligning the folded edges, re-fold the strip in half, and press again. Attach in the same way as for ready-made bias binding.

Picot edging

Fold the raw edge of the fabric over to the wrong side by ⅜ in./1 cm (or whatever seam allowance is stated). Steam press in a crisp fold. Machine stitch along the edge, using small zigzag stitches, guiding the needle of your sewing machine so that it falls off the fabric, wrapping the threads around the edge. Carefully trim away the seam allowance, taking extra care not to cut the thread.

Fringing, forelocks, and manes

1 For a neat and even finish, run a row of straight backstitches along the area to be fringed as a guide. Cut lengths of yarn, fold in half, and thread through the eye of a needle. Pass the threaded needle under the backstitches and pull the yarns halfway through.

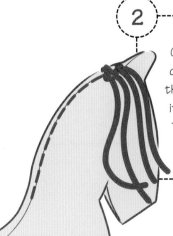

2 Carefully pull the loop in the yarn out of the eye of the needle, thread the two loose ends through it, and pull the ends to secure. Trim away any uneven ends.

Tassels and tails

1

Cut a square of medium-weight card—the size being equal to the length you want your tassel to be—with a slot inside, ¾ in. (2 cm) down from the top edge and open at one end.

2

Place a strand of yarn securely across the top edge of the square, fixing it temporarily in place with small pieces of adhesive tape, and start winding yarn vertically round it until you have the desired fullness.

3

Slip another strand of yarn in and out of the slot, wrap it round the wound yarn, and tie securely in a double knot.

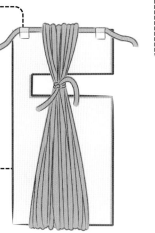

4

Tie the strand of yarn at the top of the square in a double knot to secure the top of the wound yarn. Using a pair of sharp scissors, cut the wound yarn at the bottom of the square, slide the tassel off the card, and trim away any uneven ends.

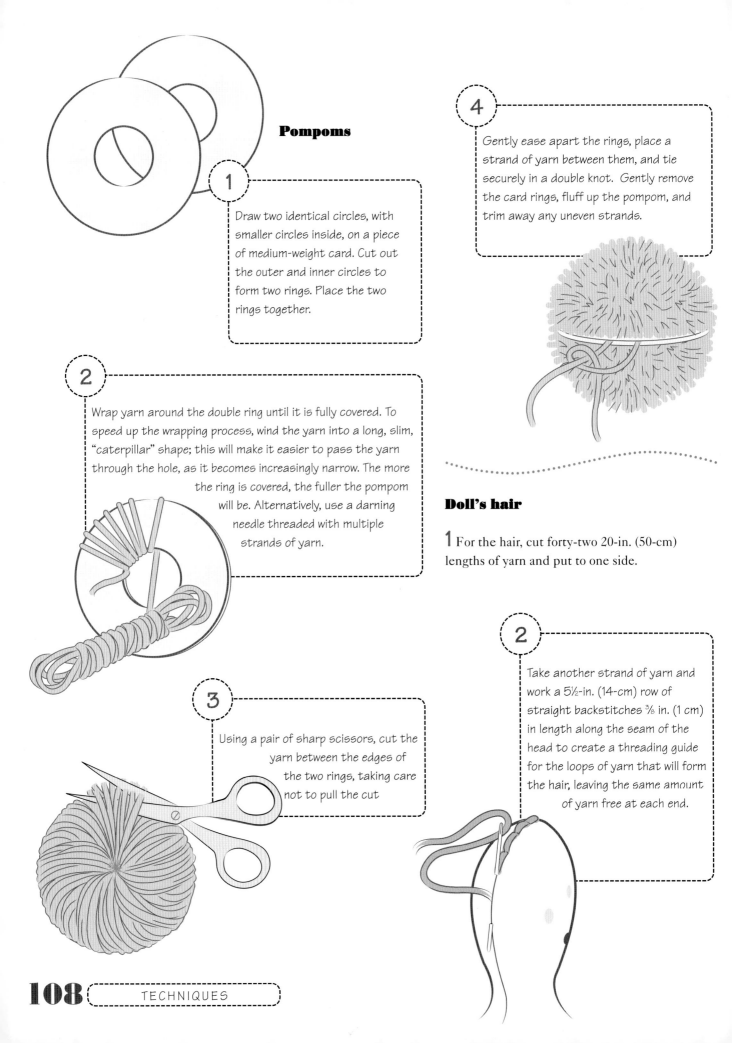

Pompoms

1 Draw two identical circles, with smaller circles inside, on a piece of medium-weight card. Cut out the outer and inner circles to form two rings. Place the two rings together.

2 Wrap yarn around the double ring until it is fully covered. To speed up the wrapping process, wind the yarn into a long, slim, "caterpillar" shape; this will make it easier to pass the yarn through the hole, as it becomes increasingly narrow. The more the ring is covered, the fuller the pompom will be. Alternatively, use a darning needle threaded with multiple strands of yarn.

3 Using a pair of sharp scissors, cut the yarn between the edges of the two rings, taking care not to pull the cut

4 Gently ease apart the rings, place a strand of yarn between them, and tie securely in a double knot. Gently remove the card rings, fluff up the pompom, and trim away any uneven strands.

Doll's hair

1 For the hair, cut forty-two 20-in. (50-cm) lengths of yarn and put to one side.

2 Take another strand of yarn and work a 5½-in. (14-cm) row of straight backstitches ⅜ in. (1 cm) in length along the seam of the head to create a threading guide for the loops of yarn that will form the hair, leaving the same amount of yarn free at each end.

3

Take one pre-cut strand of yarn, fold it in half, and thread it through the eye of a darning needle. Pass the needle under a backstitch, pull the yarn halfway, carefully pull the loop in the yarn out of the eye of the needle, thread the two loose ends through it, and pull the ends to secure. Repeat twice, using a new strand of yarn each time and passing the needle under the same backstitch. Continue until you come to the end of the row of backstitching.

6

Working outward, left and right, attach four more braids on each side of the central two in the same way. Wrap the four remaining braids (two at the lower left and two at the lower right of the head) toward the center of the back neck, and tie all the braids together in a bunch with a secure double knot.

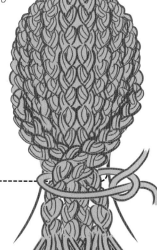

4

Take the three doubled strands of yarn that you looped under the first backstitch in the previous step, along with the first loose end of yarn left in Step 2, and braid (plait) them together. Repeat with the remaining strands of doubled yarn.

7

Cut three 40-in. (100-cm) lengths of yarn, fold each length in half, braid together to form a single braid, and knot each end securely. Hand stitch the braid to the head, following the seamline of the head and covering the row of backstitching worked in Step 2.

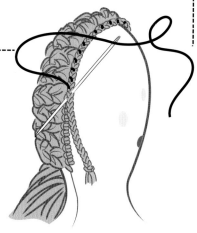

5

Place the doll face down on your work surface, lay the two central braids (plaits) down the center back of the head, and handstitch together, to the back of the head and to the base of the neck.

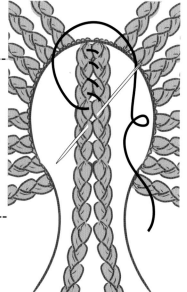

Suppliers

North America

A.C. Moore
Stores nationwide
1-888-226-6673
www.acmoore.com

A. H. Mercantile Co.
1295 E Vista Way, Ste 336
Vista, CA 92084
760-726-3355
www.ahmercantile.com

Amy Butler
www.amybutler.com

B.B. Bargoons
8201 Keele Street
Concord, ON L4K 1Z4
1-800-665-9227
www.bbbargoons.com

Britex Fabrics
146 Geary Street
San Francisco, CA 94108
415-392 2910
www.britexfabrics.com

Buy Fabrics
8967 Rand Ave
Daphne, Al 36526
877-625-2889
www.buyfabrics.com

Cia's Palette
4155 Grand Ave S
Minneapolis, MN 55409
612-229-5227
www.ciaspalette.com

Crafts, etc.
1-800-888-0321
www.craftsetc.com
Online store.

Denver Fabrics
10490 Baur Blvd. St.
St. Louis, MO 63132
1-800-468-0602
www.denverfabrics.com

Discount Fabrics USA
108 N. Carroll St.
Thurmont, MD 21788
301-271-2266
www.discountfabricsusacorp.com

FabDir.com
www.fabdir.com
The Internet's largest fabric store directory.

Fabricland/Fabricville
www.fabricland.com
www.fabricville.com
Over 170 stores in Canada.

J & O Fabrics
9401 Rt. 130
Pennsauken, NJ 08110
856-663-2121
www.jandofabrics.com

Hobby Lobby
Stores nationwide
www.hobbylobby.com

Jo-Ann Fabric and Craft Store
1-888-739-4120
www.joann.com
Stores nationwide.

Lucy's Fabrics
103 S. College Street
Anna, TX 75409
866-544-5829
www.lucysfabrics.com

Michaels
1-800-642-4235
www.michaels.com
Stores nationwide.

Purl Patchwork
147 Sullivan Street
New York, NY 10012
00 1 212 420 8798
www.purlsoho.com

Reprodepot Fabrics
413-527-4047
www.reprodepotfabrics.com

Tinsel Trading Company
47 West 38th Street
New York, NY 10018
212-730-1030
www.tinseltrading.com

Vogue Fabrics
718-732 Main Street
Evanston, IL 60202
847-864-9600
www.voguefabricstore.com

Wazoodle
2–9 Heritage Road
Markham, ON L3P 1M3
1-866-473-4628
www.wazoodle.com

Z and S Fabrics
681 S. Muddy Creek Road
Denver, PA 17157
717-336-4026
www.zandsfabrics.com

UK

Alexander Furnishings
51-61 Wigmore Street
London W1U 1PU
020 7935 1678

Borovick's
16 Berwick Street
London W1F 0HP
020 7437 2180
www.borovickfabricsltd.co.uk

The Cloth House
47 Berwick Street
London W1F 8SJ
020 7437 5155
www.clothhouse.com

Cloud Cuckoo Land
6 Charlton Place
London N1 8AJ
020 7354 3141

Dreamtime
6 Pierrepoint Row
Camden Passage
London N1 8EF

John Lewis
Oxford Street
London W1A 1EX
020 7629 7711
www.johnlewis.com

Kleins
5 Noel Street
London W1F 8GD
020 7437 6162
www.kleins.co.uk

Liberty
Regent Street
London W1
020 7734 1234
www.liberty.co.uk

Loop
41 Cross Street
London N1 2BB
020 7288 1160
www.loopknitting.com

MacCulloch & Wallis
25-26 Dering Street
London W15 1AT
020 7629 0311
www.macculloch-wallis.co.uk

The Make Lounge
49-51 Barnsbury Street
London N1 1PT
020 7609 0275
www.themakelounge.com

Past Caring
54 Essex Road
London N1 8LR

Sew Fantastic
107 Essex Road
London N1 2SL
020 7226 2725

Shock & Soul
46 Essex Road
London N1 8LN
020 7704 6572
www.shockandsoul.co.uk

VV Rouleaux
102 Marylebone Lane
London W1U 2QD
020 7224 5179
www.vvrouleaux.com

Spain

Almacenes Cobian
2 Plaza Pontejos
28012 Madrid
00 34 91 522 25 25
www.almacenescobian.es
*The best haberdashery on
the planet!*

Megino
12 Calle Corredera Alta de
San Pablo
28004 Madrid
00 34 91 522 64 50
www.megino.net

France

Les Coupons de Saint-Pierre
1 place Saint-Pierre
75018 Paris
00 33 1 42 52 10 79

La Droguerie
9 & 11 rue du Jour
75001 Paris
00 33 1 45 08 93 27
www.ladroguerie.com

Entrée des Fournisseurs
8 rue des Francs Bourgeois
75003 Paris
00 33 1 48 87 58 98
www.entreedesfournisseurs.com

Le Rouvray
3 rue de la Bûcherie
75005 Paris
00 33 1 43 25 00 45
www.lerouvay.com

Tissus Reine
3-5 place Saint-Pierre
75018 Paris
00 33 1 46 06 02 31
www.tissus-reine.com

Les Touristes
17 rue des Blancs Manteaux
75004 Paris
00 33 1 42 72 10 84
www.lestouristes.eu

Acknowledgments

I would like to thank everyone who worked on this book, especially Kate Simunek for the adorable and wonderfully animated illustrations, Emma Mitchell for the lovely photography, and Luis Peral who brought my toys to life and captured the mood I wanted. Thank you to my editor Sarah Hoggett for her essential contribution and to Elizabeth Healey for her great design. At CICO Books, a special thank you to Cindy Richards for her enthusiasm and Pete Jorgensen for all his hard work. A big thank you to all the location owners who made my eclectic bunch of creatures feel right at home!

And of course, thank you Mum, without whom this book would not have been possible.

Index